LOVING GOD
WHATEVER

LOVING GOD
WHATEVER

Through the Year with Sister Jane
Community of the Sisters of the Love of God

edited by

Jim Cotter

&

Sister Avis Mary SLG

CAIRNS PUBLICATIONS
HARLECH
in association with the
SISTERS OF THE LOVE OF GOD
OXFORD
in their centenary year
2006

ISBN 1 870652 45 2

CAIRNS PUBLICATIONS
Dwylan, Stryd Fawr, Harlech, Gwynedd LL46 2YA

www.cottercairns.co.uk
jim@cottercairns.co.uk

Typeset in Monotype Baskerville by
Strathmore Publishing Services, London EC1

CONTENTS

FOREWORD

by
Mother Rosemary SLG

I defy anyone to stick rigidly to the daily diet this splendid book prescribes for the reader – nuggets of Jane are altogether too more-ish for that! I have been enjoying browsing about, reading a long sequence of days or dipping in and out, sensing how the underlying themes cohere or, just when I'm getting a handle on them, are shattered or challenged by a joke or wry aside. They separate and re-form, like patterns in a jogged kaleidoscope.

And yet there is sense too, if you have the discipline and perseverance, in taking it as it comes. Our big commitments are lived out inch by inch, day in day out, and step by step. Speaking of her own experience of life-long commitment to God by monastic vows, Sr Jane used the image of a stout hawser composed of many strands: as life goes on, she said, more and more strands are woven in, a succession of little things which anchor one's life more and more securely in God. Life in a community such as ours is mostly unspectacular, even trivial, but the ordinary issues which crop up in our daily life are still the basic human ones: God, death, love and – Sr Jane was clear on this – 'a sense of sin', things being awry and out of tune, but 'dear God' with us at every point, to redeem and transform. I think that readers will quickly realize that her words are not glib or glibly spoken. As Robert Runcie said of her, "There is a streak of natural scepticism in her character which makes her words of faith and fortitude still accessible to those who find it hard to believe," though she is too interested in people as they are to want to foist her views upon them. Rather, her words can speak to our condition and, when they do, give hope and a practical way forward. I know one man to whom she said, "We cannot know for sure if God is Love, but we can live *as if* he is anyway" – and that has been his stout hawser ever since.

So I hope that some will find an invitation in these pages to go slowly, not gobbling, taking a day at a time, an extract at a time for a whole year, and if you do choose to do that – I wonder what the effect will be.

We owe a debt of gratitude to Jim Cotter and Sr Avis Mary, and to Sr Isabel too, for putting together this volume and making such an apt and welcome contribution to our centenary year. It is an act of love and friendship which Sr Jane's friends will especially appreciate, and which will surely make her fresh friends too. It is being published in the same spirit that David Lowe republished in 1980 *Letters of Spiritual Direction* by the Abbé de Tourville; and as Sr Jane has something in common with de Tourville, and relished his letters, I will conclude by echoing and applying here what Hugh Maycock, our chaplain at Burwash, said then.

> Readers of these extracts will learn to laugh at their own hurly-burly and to refrain from taking themselves so seriously. They will learn to rejoice in, and depend more and more upon God's unfaltering love for them, and God's intention to give them eternal happiness and fun in heaven.

That sounds like something for all of us, and a good way to mark and celebrate the first one hundred years of the Sisters of the Love of God.

MOTHER ROSEMARY SLG
Mardi Gras 2006

MEMOIR

by

Sister Isabel SLG

How do you 'remember' a person who was an important part of your life for forty years? The readers of this book have no doubt had a good deal of practice in such remembering. Dido's lament in Purcell's opera, "When I am laid in earth, remember me," or Walter de la Mare's, "And when I crumble, who will remember this lady of the West Country?" both express the baffled longing to grasp the ultimate meaning of bonds between living persons and those who have disappeared beyond their reach and beyond hope of recovery, of which we all know something. Jane did not, at least to my knowledge, ever ask to be remembered; but for those of her Sisters who knew her – fewer now than in 1995 but still including some remnants who shared her agonizing and hilarious Novitiate years, as well as those who cared for her in illness and death – everything around us, our chapel, refectory, garden, chapter house, kitchen – is thick with memories, ready to be recalled whenever we will, and often enough surfacing unsought.

Such memories are on one hand collective, for Jane was for some fourteen years as our Rule puts it, "more than anyone else responsible for the maintenance and exposition of the distinctive spirit of the Community". Like any other of its members, she had nothing but the person she was to bring to her vocation or to her office as Reverend Mother. But the same was true of what she brought to each of her personal relationships, within the Community and far beyond it, as the contents of this book will surely testify. The selective memories of individuals, revealing many different facets, are consonant with the wholeness of a self that was offered and risked within every encounter. For each of us it is easy enough to 'envision' – a word much relished by Jane who took a mischievous delight in using jargon – a voice, a laugh, a smile that were unique to one person, and at the same time recognizable (with a shift of circumstance) as the graver face of leadership and authority courageously shouldered.

It was while working as a librarian in the Bank of England that what Jane would often speak of later (quoting Father Hollings) as being 'drawn into the wilderness for the sake of God alone' became a summons she could no longer ignore. She was admitted as a postulant in September 1956, at almost exactly the mid-point of the Community's century. A few weeks later, sitting on the window-sill of the Novitiate with an even newer postulant who, not sure of the propriety of the question, timidly asked her how old she was, she replied, 'Oh, I'm quite a hag, twenty-nine.'

It would be idle and misleading to pretend to a privileged know-ledge of Jane's interior life, for (to take liberties with St Paul) "what woman," he asks the Corinthians, "knows the things of a woman except the spirit of the woman that is in her?" A memoir cannot avoid some superficiality and a vast ignorance. Each one of us who knew Jane knew her in a particular way. Nevertheless, it needed no great penetration nor the passage of much time for most people to see that, with all her adaptability and engaging friendliness, Jane was crucially motivated by that central precept of our Rule:

> From their first entry into the Community the Sisters shall study to develop in themselves the spirit of love, setting the well-being of their Sisters and the perfection of the Community as a whole above any personal aims or desires of their own.

It is neither to exaggerate nor to collapse into hagiography to say that for the whole of her monastic life Jane was a living embodi-ment of that precept. She was able to embody it and to enjoin it on her Sisters, because, while embracing the common life as whole-heartedly as she did, she neither "looked too good nor talked too wise" as she went about it, and because by nature as well as by grace she was lacking in selfishness.

This early grasp of sacrificial love at the core of the SLG vocation, was in one sense the logical progression from a drawing to the mys-tery of Christ's suffering that was already there. As a young woman she had gone with her mother every year in Holy Week to hear a performance of Bach's *St Matthew Passion*. As a novice she took the dedication to the Divine Compassion, and as the years went by that aspect of the Incarnate Nature became for her identified with the Cross. That "Christ died *for us* while we were yet sinners" became the leitmotif of her life, so that union with Christ, if it were ever to be attained, *must* mean union with the Crucified; and therefore, suffering, whatever form it might take, was to be – entirely without morbidity or parade – desired and welcomed. It would do less than justice to the truth of Jane, least solemn and sanctimonious of Sisters, not to stress this fundamental thirst to be identified with Christ in sacrificial love. She knew that for some of her Sisters, "King of Glory, King of Peace, I will love Thee" might best express the theme most native to their hearts, while for her and for others it was more probably "In thy most bitter Passion, my heart to share doth cry." She needed no persuasion to embrace the truth that Calvary and the Easter Garden are each the locus of the one indivisible glory to which she had dedicated her life, and she ordered it according to that conviction. It would be hard to exaggerate the influence of our founding fathers and mothers on the person Jane would become. Their teaching expounded Scripture as pre-eminently the food of contemplative adoration, and the Rule as a comprehensive programme for those who had pledged themselves to a lifetime of intercession on behalf of the world. "Prayer, observance, discipline, thought and action…This is the way, walk ye in it."

That the way was often hard was neither here nor there. Jane had certainly expected nothing else. Faced with a tough dilemma, she would choose her course of action, commenting in the tone of half-serious gloom she sometimes affected: "Well, we're called to a life of sacrifice, so it might as well be this as anything." But when the problem was someone else's, Jane exemplified something that is often to be seen in generous people, namely, that hard experience does not harden a generous heart but actually makes it more tender and understanding. She and her fellow-novices were blessed in the guidance of a Novice Mistress of rare charm and intuition who managed to enliven the rudiments of a monastic, theological and liturgical education with a fair amount of input from *The Lord of the Rings*, and who, when required to save the bacon of one or other of her charges caught in a domestic or emotional crisis, would more often than not resolve it with the therapy of laughter. Laughter was a concomitant of Jane's life at all stages, and something she really could not do without. Absence of laughter for more than a day or two was not just depressing, it was alarming, and would have to be made good quickly. She had the keenest sense of the ridiculous – in life's ironies, in situations, and in her fellow-human beings – and could muster a range of stories against herself to recount to others with that lugubrious enjoyment which invited confidences in return, and restored a perspective in which persons could thrive and grow. Her readiness to be – and be seen to be – in the same boat as her neighbour, her admonitions, firm but never lofty, uncompromising but always kind, wove the bonds of deep affection and laid foundations for the trust which, if monastic life is to remain healthy, must inevitably be put to the test from time to time.

As Reverend Mother, Jane conducted Community business from the 'red desk', a cumbrous mass of metal, allegedly bought from an army surplus store, which on her instructions was painted her favourite colour and installed in her office. Soon it was followed by a pair of forbidding black armchairs for the accommodation of visitors. A gentle and patient listener, who never interrupted with premature advice, Jane's humour, delicacy, and silence were no less part of the guidance and encouragement she gave than were her actual words. When the conversation was over, it was more often than not followed up at once by a letter. She might write as many as twelve in a day. Constantly resorted to and with a huge capacity for friendship, Jane never aspired to be a 'star' in the firmament of the wise. Essentially, she was a shy person, drawn out of the obscurity she preferred by the Community's sure instinct for the kind of leader it needed when, after nineteen years, Mother Mary Clare's outstanding term of office came to an end. Jane was not unprepared to succeed her, but as Reverend Mother, she would keep as much of that obscurity as was allowed her. In the last seven years of her life it amounted to a great deal.

By the end of her own term of office in 1988 the asthma, whose seriousness she, and others, had for too long under-estimated, had become very frightening and almost uncontrollable. Drastically restricted in breathing and mobility as she was, the essentials of the person whom her sisters saw, cherished, and delighted in, remained unchanged; and at times of respite she was still able to enjoy their company, when sanctioned by a ponderous adopted cat which gradually took up permanent residence on her bed and glared balefully at anyone who presumed to enter the room. While everyone was careful not to make her laugh, communication was maintained, and became ever more precious as time ran out. Favourite books such as *The Crucified God* by Moltmann, Vanstone's *Love's Endeavour, Love's Expense*, and especially Sebastian Moore's *The Crucified is No Stranger* were re-visited, and shared; letters and notes were written. Thus vigilance and diligent nursing helped to prolong for a few years a very fragile life. But very early on a cold spring morning, the Feast of St Patrick, Jane received the summons she had waited for with such grace and fortitude. Nobody knows at exactly what moment it came, but as the Community heard the tolling bell, and took their places in Chapel for the Prayers, everyone knew with certainty that "a condition of complete simplicity, costing not less than everything," had been met in full.

SISTER ISABEL SLG
Fairacres, February 2006

PREFACE

Sister Jane, who died in 1995, was Mother of the Community of the Sisters of the Love of God from 1973–1988. One duty which never came easily to her was to give a formal 'chapter charge' to her Sisters each year, and to write a message for each issue of the *Fairacres Chronicle*. Like most of us, she was more relaxed – and revealing – when she was writing informally, not least to those many people who drank deep of her wisdom. Selections from all these occasional pieces appear in this book, along with a few extracts from other talks and from her own marginal notes on the Community's rule of life. There has been a little light editing for the sake of clarity and for ease of pondering, e.g. some of the longer sentences have been split into two or three.

The more formal quotations suited one possible title, *Pledged to God*, but that sounded too solemn. The less formal items suited another, *Bless this Mess*. And that sounded rather flippant for a limited-edition gift book. Could a title be found that would honour both the seriousness of her commitment and the lightheartedness with which she was learning to regard herself? I hope that *Loving God Whatever* is good enough.

The Community graciously and trustingly gave me access to much of the Sister Jane archive, and for Sister Avis Mary's help in this I am particularly grateful – as I am to Mother Rosemary for her Foreword and to Sister Isabel for her Memoir. My thanks are also due to those of Sister Jane's correspondents who lent me the letters they had received and gave me permission to quote from them.

Having drafted the selections, I had to work out how to present them. Jane was never a systematic thinker or writer, and so it didn't feel right to lump together the chapter charges, then the messages, then the letters. Nor did an arrangement by themes, not least because there were considerable overlaps, even in the shorter items. And references to seasons, either meteorological or liturgical, are

few. Then, given that the draft manuscript had a sequence of num-
bered items, 1–377 (allowing for a few editorial cuts to bring the
total down to 366), I thought, Why not by lot? We do well not to
separate too much serious pondering from the laughter that keeps
things in proportion. And I recalled one of Jane's favourite lines in
her letters, at times when either she or a correspondent was stuck
with a difficulty for which there was no apparent way through, "So
wot?" (The deliberate mis-spelling was typically self-deprecating.)

So, the numbers were listed, the paper cut, the pieces folded and
put into a box. Halfway through this game of editorial bingo I was
struck by how ludicrous the process felt, though fortunately the
rough and ready mix seemed to be working. Then, in my mind's
ear, I heard a chuckle from Jane, and I couldn't help laughing out
loud. It cheered me through what was fast becoming a laboursome
chore. ("So wot?")

Well, I think that Jane would, perhaps secretly, have been
pleased to see this book in print, maybe also chuffed that it was
being published as part of the centenary celebrations of the Community. And I want to end this Preface by expressing my own quiet
gratitude for the hospitality and wisdom of the Sisters of the Love
of God ever since I was overwhelmed by the density of the silence
in the chapel at Boxmoor, Hemel Hempstead, in the autumn of
1977. I think it was on the the sixth of August 1978, the Feast of the
Transfiguration – always a favourite of mine – that I first met
Mother Jane, as she then was, in the garden at Fairacres in Oxford.
For a few years I made an annual retreat in raw December at Bede
House near Staplehurst in Kent, and towards the end of the first
week there I remember sitting bolt upright one afternoon and
realizing that I had rarely felt so *loved* as I had that week by the
Sisters. I haven't a clue – and probably they don't either – about
how that happened. It was the very opposite of intrusive and
hearty. It was simply there, given out of the love of God of their
dedication. Thank you, Sisters of the Love of God.

Oh yes, I do have to admit that I tweaked the dates given to a
few items. There are a couple that specifically mention Christmas,
there is an appropriate one for All Souls' Day, and I couldn't resist

a piece on humour for the Feast of Fools on the first of April. And
I daresay there'll be a bit of shuffling at proof stage of this book's
production, so that the occasional words and lines don't look lonely
at top or bottom of a page.

JIM COTTER
Harlech, October 2005

…as in so many aspects of our life, the future is splendidly uncertain. Nothing is secure, except God; we have no abiding city. We are called into the wilderness to be perpetual pilgrims, and although Father Hollings and his few pious ladies would undoubtedly blink somewhat to find themselves among us now, I trust they would not disinherit us.

from Mother Jane's
fourth chapter charge in 1976

1 January   Patience, which allows people to change and situations
to evolve and work themselves out; hope, which knows that time
must eventually pass and that successive crises have been lived
through before, both globally and personally; and a sense of the
ridiculous which can keep things in proportion and help us to
apply in daily life the knowledge that God matters most to us all:
these necessary virtues enable us to be open to surprises and ready
for risks.

2 January   I know what you mean about not wanting to pray. But
I suppose that is ultimately as irrelevant as those rare occasions
when one is 'caught' in prayer and wants to stay beyond the allot-
ted time. Neither is what really matters. What *does* matter is what
God is doing. It is all his business: ours is to have the humility to
consent, or to want to consent, to this.

3 January   I believe that…growth in…vulnerability and dependence is what our vocation to a life of prayer is all about, and…if as
a community we are feeling the need for more stretches of prayer
and times of solitude…it is for such growth that we need them. We
have nothing to give God but the use he can make of us, and it is
only in so far as we are ready to be 'hit' by whatever aspect of evil
needs to be absorbed and neutralized through us, that we can claim
to be really given to him.

4 January   Loving God is here and now its own reward.

5 January   Love means being alongside, in companionship: rejoicing with or suffering helplessly with – not instead of – the beloved,
and delighting in the other as a person.

6 January   Because modern technology and the amazing recent
developments of science indicate the possibility of our advancing
indefinitely in understanding and control of life and environment,
we risk losing that capacity to expect the unexpected which charac-
terizes the humility essential for being fully human.

7 January   …it is not what we do so much as the way we are which God uses.

8 January   …the important thing is to be faithful to our appointed times of 'sheer prayer' when, because we are trying to live in a 'free response of love' to him, we place ourselves before God in openness and readiness to give and receive. How frequently, though, these times are cluttered up with our concerns about the particular responsibilities that are engaging us at the moment, or the hard work entailed in trying to know ourselves better so that we can consciously bring more to God. Our suffering and our offering of the 'clutter' is, surely, accepted by God in his mercy as prayer.

9 January   …inspirational words…must be earthed in the reality of everyday life so that in the rough and tumble of situations beyond our control and capacity to cope they are still what we try to live by.

10 January   …in acknowledging that there is so much that we cannot know because we are finite, we can nevertheless be pretty sure of everything being contained in the net of love. I'm never 'absolutely' sure, because somehow I acknowledge fewer and fewer absolutes, don't you?

11 January   [When ill during a visit to Australia] …I wallow in every creature comfort, and friendly people, and a lot of fun, and nice letters…and many giggles with God, whom I certainly don't doubt even if I haven't any silence of my own, or congenial spirituality, in which to 'experience' him.

12 January   I should prefer to think of community life as a dynamic dance rather than as a static city, for I think God makes us responsible for weaving in and out of positions among ourselves, and relationships in his Kingdom are in perpetual motion.

13 January   All too often it seems that we are asked to stay with the perplexity and ambiguity of unquenched light in undisposed darkness. In a grey situation, it can happen that the only response is a grey one, and part of our prayer must be our willingness to accept the pain of compromise and helplessness that comes from our encounters with persons and circumstances as they actually are.

14 January   Somehow the sort of God that Jesus reveals is so superabundantly wonderful that I'm happy to have had the idea of him. I do think that a God who loves the world so much that he becomes human, and lives and dies for love of it, is beyond our own fabrication, don't you? I was struck the other day by the full implication of Colossians 1.24–27 (it's mentioned in chapter 2 of our Rule), that one function of the members of Christ's body the Church is to enable him to go on suffering afflictions in the way he did when he was incarnate. Isn't it amazing how one (this one, anyway) suddenly 'sees' the obvious?

15 January   …we are not called primarily to condemn or condone by pontificating about principles but to live the reality of the Love of God in particular circumstances as we meet them.

16 January   God is in the mess and pioneers go down into it with him. And we can't be pulled up to perfection by expertise, self-effort, good works, or righteousness.

17 January   Perhaps redemption and transfiguration are simultaneous with creation, except that, I suppose, it's all outside time. So as we, collectively and individually, trudge through life (which is of course indisputably *marvellous* as well as tragic!) we can know that however ghastly and unbelievable general and particular situations are, and however intransigent, somehow in ways we can never understand or articulate we know that "All shall be well," because God's been there and is there. This seems to me the heart of what Christianity has to offer.

18 January   I suppose the beastliness of politics is to some extent a game, which diffuses the aggression which otherwise becomes nationalism, racism, and all the other awful -isms that are so rampant. I find it increasingly important to remind other people *and* myself that one doesn't do any good anywhere by getting sucked into the horrors that are so vivid and ubiquitous, but that it's terribly important to remember all that's *positive* in creation, including humans, and to remember the countless millions who *are* praying, and thinking God-ward in however unrecognizable a way.

19 January   As the Desert Fathers well knew, our life with God is in and through one another. So it will be in the impactedness brought about by enclosure (and this, surely, is what that much disputed 'privilege' is mainly about) that the truth of who we are is revealed. We are not here to become 'nice' people or even, in our estimation, 'whole' people. These terms are relative, and our primary purpose is to become more and more God's people.

20 January   For the last few days I've been basking in a very pleasant conviction that God is more real than me. Obvious, but I'm not often sure of it.

21 January   For each of us individually, and for the Community as a whole, our life is bogus unless the central factor in it is the experience (of which we may or may not be aware) of open, empty givenness to God. Probably my words are not those you would choose, but you will know what I mean. It is in our own prayer, trying to receive God as he is and not as we suppose him, that we shall learn the heart of what we need to about making relationships, finding and taking responsibility for our selves, formulating and defending principles, etc.; and unless anything we do or say or think flows out from and back to that central God-wardness, we are betraying him and the world we are here to serve. We are called to "have the whole being set on God", and any deviation from this is lack of love and the basic root of sin, whatever form the fruit of it may take.

22 January Living together closely, as we do, does not solve communication problems. We work and eat in silence, and there is no place like a silent community for generating misunderstanding and incomprehension.

Every reader of a written notice is likely to interpret it differently, and the chances are that the writer's intention will be missed by all. We know that the problem is not unique to SLG, and we can live with it and laugh at ourselves. We are a small example of the basic incapacity of one human being really to understand another. But the truth of the Incarnation brings hope! For God has done for each of us what we cannot do for one another: he has got inside our skins.

23 January After all, it's only each of us who imposes upon ourselves the assumption that we've got to 'get it right'. But what matters is the 'going with the grain' of what actually is – not resisting it in order to get things the way *I* think, but fitting in with what's possible so that 'the best way' can peacefully evolve.

24 January I love the liturgical seasons more and more, although I take such little part in their observance. I also love the spring, and the SUN always!

25 January I know that my way of putting things about vocation isn't with the same emphases that all would wish, but I do know that none of us can say anything real except out of her own experience. And I think what I *do* believe to be true is that the Community can be used by God and make sense to the lonely people who come here, men and women, ordained and lay, married and single. All seem to have the sort of emptiness at the centre which we know too and can make sense of in terms of "the power of his resurrection and the fellowship of his sufferings". And we can continue to shed abroad "the love wherein He has loved us" only if we hold to and try to follow Father Hollings' original intention that the Community should be ready to follow Jesus into the wilderness in our personal and corporate life and prayer.

26 January   ...silence is often terrifying. We can't smugly pretend we always want to worship.

27 January   I was talking to another sister about 'prayer for guidance' in general, and she said she thought God says to us: "You choose and I'll be with you." This seems to me to make a lot of sense. I'm sure it's true, too. The things that really matter in life are about *loving* – God and people, who are inseparable, of course, and not the mountainous things and the immediate decisions and disasters that always loom so large.

28 January   Jesus went the way of the Cross in love, forgiving even *in extremis,* and shows that it is the nature of God to go through the slings and arrows of any life, redeeming through love and affirming an ultimate 'rightness' beyond our imaginings.

29 January   Each of us individually, in God's good time, is impelled to realize that unless we live by faith, day by day laying hold upon fresh aspects of the original leap which landed us here, we shall be submerged. For 'the whole life to become prayer' is not a far-off ideal to be attained by the few: it is a necessity of survival for us all, and for the humankind we represent.

30 January   I find that for me, getting nearer to death means not increasing holiness but a dawning awareness of being taken out of time. I find this very interesting and *Four Quartet*-ish.
[A reference to T. S. Eliot's sequence of poems, *Four Quartets*]

31 January   Listening to the Terce antiphon this morning, I wondered what, for example, the average resident of Fairacres Road would make of: "The days of penitence are come to us for the redemption of our sins and the saving of our souls." I certainly wish we could express more nearly – though never adequately – the reality of God's love (which does not consist in making us comfy) and its embracing of the whole of Creation.

1 February Bodily appetites, indeed, can be for many of us a cause of humiliation and discomfort. But perhaps acceptance of this mortification, of our helplessness and sense of failure, brings us nearer to God, for he is always to be found in the outcast, disreputable parts of ourselves as well as of our society...

2 February Christian teaching tends to imply that if you make a friend of Jesus he will look after you. Whereas he really says: As the Father has sent me, I also send you – to be immersed in the human condition for good or for ill, and to lay down your life for the sake of the world.

3 February Penitence is not so much fretting about one's personal wrongdoing as a lively sense of personal concern in the sin of the world.

4 February To my mind our corporate reluctance (among ourselves – I've seldom known us show discourtesy) in regard to 'visitors' in the abstract is healthy. As soon as any of us makes a real encounter with someone else as a person, we cease to doubt the rightness of their coming. It is not our vocation to make hospitality an apostolate, or even, in the Benedictine tradition, "to extend it to the stranger as to Christ". Rather, ours is, I believe, the Carmelite way of sharing what we have got with others who are on the same spiritual pilgrimage.

5 February If God is whom I love and believe him to be, he won't give me 'comfort'. But that fact is in itself the most supreme comfort!

6 February ...as in so many aspects of our life, the future is splendidly uncertain; nothing is secure, except God; we have no abiding city. We are called into the wilderness to be perpetual pilgrims, and although Father Hollings and his few pious ladies would undoubtedly blink somewhat to find themselves among us now, I trust they would not disinherit us.

7 February   As to your unorthodox Christianity, well, a lot of us
have moved from the 'simple acceptance' faith that brought us to
respond to vocation. Doing that thing is itself a very much more
complex procedure for today's postulants than it was for me. When
she was washing me the other day, the Infirmarian said, "I think
Mother is sometimes surprised by the atheism of her sisters." I said,
after thought, "I believe passionately and profoundly in God: it's
'religion' I can't be doing with." And yet, of course, that has meant
everything to me in years past, and I'm unfailingly grateful. Even
now, when I'm amazed at the acceptance by my sisters of my
unconcealed lack of religious practices, and delight at being not
expected to participate in them, I need some sort of framework for
my little life, and I 'think' the Gradual Psalms I know by heart
(Book of Common Prayer version) when I have my ruminative
snoozes that punctuate my day.

8 February   Jesus had a ruthless regard for reality, and went
through life stripped of the protection of illusions. The man whom
we meet in the Gospels is free from preconceptions and prejudice
and, above all, from self-deception.

9 February   …the tradition of the Community is that no sister shall
remain overlong in any one occupation, or be regarded by herself
or others as indispensable. None of us is unmindful of the cost of
letting go, and indeed we should not do any job properly unless we
became thoroughly involved in it. Change is always inconvenient
and uncomfortable, but it is an integral and essential part of that
'divine movement' ensuring that we live as strangers and pilgrims,
having no abiding possessions or resting place.

10 February   In every area of life there is a balance of change and
permanence. Each season in nature, as well as in the Church's year,
is new and old, different and the same. There are cycles in history
and patterns in the universe, and in our own lives we sometimes
experience a sense of 'having been there before' in place and time.

11 February [On a sentence attributed to J. H. Oldham: "We are each of us infinitely responsible for our own infinitesimal bit of reality."] Each successive *now* is the 'infinitesimal bit of reality' for which we have 'infinite responsibility'. That responsibility requires each of us an integrity of response to the God who has brought us here, which may well involve clashes of opinion and principle among us.

12 February We must be prepared to have our being essentially in a narrow place with no room for manoeuvre...not because we are hedged around with rules and prohibitions, but because it is the inescapability of being beholden to our Community that provides the constriction which is the only means to an expansion in the end.

13 February If we are to pray for the world, we have got to be exposed: sometimes this means going further out, against our will; sometimes it means drawing further in to face what is in ourselves, also against our will.

14 February As always, we alone are responsible for accepting or rejecting God's challenge; but the more we are ready to take the consequences, at every level of experience, of being totally exposed to each present moment, the more sensitive we shall become – but not always for our own greater comfort. St Ignatius Loyola, standing in spiritual poverty before God, found that his respect for the Creator extended to all creatures. Going out to them in loving humility, he found God himself to be the source of glory in them. How uncommon such an attitude would be in today's world, and how many conflicts of opinion would be constructive and fruitful instead of the reverse if those concerned had respect for one another's good faith and integrity.

15 February The newness of Christianity is the proclamation that the coming of God's Kingdom consists not in a 'role reversal' so that the underdog becomes the upper dog and vice versa, but in the realization of Jesus' command to love one another.

16 February   Our prayer is given-ness in total availability to God. We don't need to understand.

17 February   God respects each one of us as a mystery and we must do the same.

18 February   Goodness! Sixty-five is *young* still! Or, well, *elderly*, but not old. And I reckon that active passivity is a most valuable aspect of life. One is so fortunate to have and to recognize the opportunity for it, though our instinct for 'human doing' rather than 'human being' makes it hard not to feel guilty about apparent uselessness.

19 February   …first and foremost we are a pilgrim people…we cannot settle down to the comfortable; we must be always moving on, and always exposed: at the mercy of God, and in that mercy finding all we need. This involves being in close touch with our contemporary world, at a level below conscious knowledge of events – though I believe that such knowledge is in fact something required of the majority of us: receiving information can be costly, and if we accept this it will not distract our Godward attention. But much more important is a right understanding of Father Gilbert Shaw's maxim: "We are a microcosm of the macrocosm." Our Community mirrors the world in miniature. We contain within and among ourselves all the potential forces for good and evil that are in humanity, and it is for us to be open to the Spirit so that he can work through us to draw humankind to the full measure of the image and likeness of God. Our experience of the sorrows and happiness of the human condition is underpinned by 'perpetual gladness', because, if our only hope is in God, it cannot be shaken by what seems to us tragedy and disaster for others and for ourselves.

20 February   God determines for each of us the occasion and the measure of "the dark cold and empty desolation" he asks us to experience, and we do not doubt that ultimately "the wilderness and the solitary places shall be glad for them," whether or not we know it.

21 February   ...we have to be prepared to open ourselves utterly to the impingement of circumstances and people on our inmost self. This is what we instinctively try to preserve and protect, and what we must voluntarily sacrifice if we are to follow Christ in the way of the Cross. "I lay down my life of myself," said Jesus, and equally we must be disposed to do the same. For if we are minded to protect ourselves we shall do so whatever systems or structures are designed to prevent this. It is all too possible to hide behind informality, rebellion, and self-expression, or behind rigid adherence to convention, theory, and idealism. All we can know is that we must be ready to let go of everything ...not only of 'I want' but also of 'I ought'. For devotion to duty can be a subtle form of self-seeking, wanting approbation and security – and we can truly assert and build up that willingness long before we have any idea of what it will involve. This is what 'growth in holiness' is all about and why it does depend so vitally upon our relationship with one another in the monastic family.

22 February   If we have courage to admit the reality...that we can rely only on God, we are open to receive the glory which will shine into every corner of our lives and ourselves, showing up the shadows most starkly, but inflaming us with a delight in God that keeps our perspective right and helps us to accept and transcend our own and other people's shortcomings because the love of God is so much more important.

23 February   Sister N has no energy...and can't eat. So she's just waiting patiently, confident that our Lord who has been faithfully with her for nearly ninety-three years won't leave her now. I said what an important work of intercession our death should be, for we can, as it were, gather up all those who have died and are dying afraid, lonely, and unprepared. But if we are each to live fully the experience of our own death, we are very dependent on the prayer and participation of every one of our sisters. So we shall all be specially alongside Sister N in thankfulness and prayer through these coming weeks.

24 February   Really to listen to the situation we are in means silencing the clamour which is perpetually going on in most of us, protesting that things ought not to be as they are, nor should I be the sort of person I am, and all in all 'it's not fair.' When we come to the point of recognizing and accepting the facts, we can look at them objectively and make a response that is courageous because it depends on God's strength making use of our weaknesses. It often happens that when we are 'beaten down with it', we are overcome not so much by the practical difficulties that surround us as by the inner fuss we are making about imagined impossibilities.

If by listening we can discover the reality of the circumstances we are coping with – be they permanent or temporary – we can move on to the next step: to hold things without being deflected by our own or other people's desires – in other words, to 'stay with it', and to find in it the joy of the heart's desiring.

25 February   Ideally, apartness should not be a matter of defiance. We do not turn our backs on so much that is good in life through scorn or despair. Rather do we come to a fuller appreciation of the loveliness of creation and the rich potential of human personality when our field of experience is narrowed. But recognizing that in every sphere, as William Blake said, joy is to be kissed as it flies, the message proclaimed by those in religious life – described in a recent article in *The Times* as "a mobile force of consecrated eccentrics" – is that the realities worth living and dying for cannot be comprehended by senses or intellect alone, and that humankind is not made for self-fulfilment in enjoyment or achievement, but for glory: the glory known by the Son with the Father before the world was; the glory of a love that comes to its fulness by the way of the Cross and no other.

26 February   I used to find that one had just to give one's attention to 'the next thing to be done' (even if one felt one had made a wrong choice about what that was) and trust that the situation and/or one's disposition would change. Of course it's very important, isn't it, to remember that one is as just as much given to God when life seems all agley as when things feel nicely under control (if that is ever the case). Our great guru, Father Gilbert Shaw, used to teach us to pray: "Here's me – what a mess," and that is the spirit in which I have lived and do live.

27 February [On being re-elected as Mother of the Community] It was really hilarious as I was listed to read the Night Office lesson last night, and it was Job cursing the day of his birth in no uncertain terms. Sr N said she'd never heard me read with such conviction. Really one has to laugh, it's the only thing to do, and thank God SLG can and does.

28 February "*Ich will hier bei Dir stehen.*" ["I want to stand here, beside you" – from an additional verse of the hymn 'O sacred head sore wounded', sung at Sister Jane's funeral.] There is all the difference in the world between a sentimental expression of this that gives *me* pleasure…and an involuntary miniscule experience of being there in an impossible, unbearable, and unavoidable situation.

29 February In the plane I had to fill in a questionnaire for travellers, and I expect I've floored the computers by answering: *What is your profession?* Sister in Religion. *What is your job?* Mother General. *What is the main purpose of your organization?* To live a life of prayer.

1 March No one should minimize the solemnity, loneliness, and hard cost of death; but surely we cannot doubt that there is some element of continuity when a loved soul is taken by its 'Father for eternity' into the fuller organization of a fellowship glimpsed, perhaps unwittingly, during life on earth.

2 March There is so much grieving in life that I cannot believe our bereavements (not only of persons) are not potentially positive rather than enduringly painful.

3 March   About your 'Godlessness'. I quite agree that trite remarks about aridity and dark nights don't help, but I have found something that *can't* 'come and go' with my feelings. And that is the *fact* of having glimpsed the mind-blowing love of God as shown in Jesus Christ. The *glimpse* is 'mine to keep'. It may be delusion; it may not do me a shred of good; but it's worth dying and even living for, I think.

4 March   The intercessory life…is the willingness to be exposed to awareness of all aspects of the human condition, the living out of whatever is the reality for us at any given time *as consciously as possible*.

5 March   Why have we been bonded together so that the consecration which ties us to God in a voluntary commitment more compelling than any number of high walls and taboos would be, also forces us into an awareness of arid impingement on one another which constantly threatens our wished-for autonomy? The answer, briefly, seems to me to be: so that we shall look beyond ourselves and know at first hand, and at grass root level, something of the consequences of division, strife, and what Father Alan Harrison has referred to as 'memorials to hatred' in the world; and so that we should give ourselves uncompromisingly to be used in God's purposes of healing and new growth. This is not a demand to be trifled with, and one feels increasingly that opportunities lost will not be given again.

6 March   I become more and more convinced that relationship pertains to the very essence of being human, and, as such, is divine and eternal.

7 March   I find I can quite happily put up with other sisters believing and subscribing to things I don't, because somehow I don't *dis*believe, I just don't believe, if you see what I mean. I know that God is huge and mysterious enough to encompass it all.

8 March We have to be humble to admit that we cannot and do not need to understand the mind of God. What humanity has been and is still learning through the birth of Jesus nearly two thousand years ago is that we are invited, not compelled, to love God. He risks our refusal but never gives us up. If we struggle beyond our natural concepts of what constitutes happiness for humankind, in the midst of the anguished divisions and losses we experience, we will find assurances of eternal harmony.

9 March Strangely, for me the 'psychological' terminology makes much more impact than the 'spiritual'. So while I could cerebrally accept the idea of the indwelling Christ, I could suppose he was in everyone (though I didn't do much about it), but never in *me*. So it's only with the realization of his being the true self of everyone (including me – because I'm *very* painfully aware of my huge ego!), that I've been able to imagine the possibility of loving myself. As you say, we find it hard to practise what we preach, and apply to ourselves what we believe for others.

10 March "I did know thee in the wilderness, in the land of great drought," says the Lord to his people through the prophet Hosea. In all his dealings with humankind from the beginning, he has repeatedly called some aside for direct confrontation with himself. Usually this has involved leaving behind the luxuries of life – and, judging by God's displeasure with Moses and the Israelites at Meribah, sometimes necessities as well. Always it has meant the transcending of mere space/time existence, not to deny its validity, but in order to affirm the eternal dimension 'in all things and above all things'.

11 March I'm sure that's what life with and for God is all about: 'keeping on keeping on' because of a commitment freely made in love and to Love, whatever I 'think' or 'feel' about it...surely the *point* of prayer is not 'what I can get out of it', but the giving of myself to God for whatever he wants because I love him – and know that he loves me. So above all, faithfulness in prayer undertakings matters.

12 March   Prayer is *not* something separate and solemn and boring; it's the most important ingredient of life and the best part of it: fun and enjoyment and interest, opening on to ever new and wider horizons. At least surely that's what it's meant to be. But a lot of self-centred impedimenta has to be cleared out of the way first, and that's costly and painful.

13 March   I honestly think people don't spend as much time thinking about us as we suppose they do, simply because, if they're anything like us, they are very much occupied in thinking about themselves. The 'perpetual availability' syndrome can easily lead us to the 'look at me, I'm indispensable' fallacy. I know all these pitfalls from having fallen into them, of course.

14 March   Contemplatives are called to offer their lives to God, not primarily in works, but in worship, simply after the manner of the woman with the jar of ointment, to give him the love he needs. The omnipotent God *needing* love? Surely we must find that living by love makes us less and less self-sufficient. So it is reasonable to think that the same is true in some way of God who loved us first and who teaches us that freedom, choice, and risk are intrinsic factors in the sacrificial, self-giving love he gives and requires.

15 March   Contemplation is concerned primarily with looking out-ward, not inwards. Introspection can be necessary and fruitful but for all of us there is an ever-present danger of getting bogged down in self-absorption. Self-knowledge is an important part of growth towards God, but once we have realized how far short each one of us falls of what she would like to be, we can accept the fact and get on with life because no one minds or condemns us, and we are in the best possible place, among friends. We should, of course, be more concerned with what Julian of Norwich calls "holy, marvel-ling delight in God", wonder and surprise at his creation, animate (including our sisters) – and inanimate – pleased, also, to share with others the riches of our spiritual endowment while being glad to receive from them in mutual exchange.

16 March "The love of Christ has joined us together." If we 'love' one another because of Christ it means that his mind is in us to a degree that makes us able to 'receive' one another as God does. We shall not necessarily find one another more congenial on a natural level; but we shall apprehend a little of the divine truth in our fellow human beings – and perhaps eventually even in ourselves. The element of 'letting go' is built into all our relationships by our vow of chastity, and we look for their fulfilment in our common convergence on God. We do not have to take too seriously the tiffs and traumas that sometimes fill our immediate horizon, but we do need to recognize these as part of the stuff of life and means of response to vocation. There is no situation in which we cannot pray 'God', and often when we know ourselves to be culpable and feel ashamed, as well as ill-tempered, we have got an opportunity that he can use.

17 March The days are long past when the Community was virtually sufficient unto itself and we permitted like-minded people an association with us which was primarily for their benefit. We now know very well that we need the enrichment brought to us by our fellow pilgrims travelling the same Christian way and sharing our special concern for reconciliation and a thoroughly incarnated spirituality.

Some of our closest friends have no specific 'SLG' label. But all connected with us, who often have a lonely struggle in their particular situations, can at many levels inject reality into our praying care, ensuring that it does not become idealistic and abstract, while the established Community can provide solid evidence of continuity and corporate commitment for them.

In the unity of Christ's love for all of us, we need – and share – one another.

18 March ...when I look deeper, I find that what I fear is the loss of control, of knowing where I am, of 'pulling my weight', of being seen, by others and by myself, to 'do my bit'. Perhaps God leads us to a gradual letting go of even knowing where we are –

risking 'lostness'. When I thought sometimes that I'd never breathe again, I found it best to try and breathe *out*, relaxing *into* the fear, rather than vainly gasping *in*. So, let go into the love of God, and, as you say, he'll take care of the show.

19 March   Being devoid of 'great thoughts' at this time, I'm finding more and more I believe our purpose in life to be the affirming of God in all circumstances, especially when they are unexpected, as both you and I have experienced lately. Helplessness of body seems – for me anyway – to entail numbness of spirit too, so that one has to leave even one's praying to be done by God. Somehow the willing acceptance of agnosticism at every level and in every sphere is all one can aspire to. It sounds rather negative and passive, but it's actually quite positive in experience.

20 March   People are often so pathetically grateful for what they think we give them, both individually and corporately. How tremendously humbled one can be by their gratitude, and how important it is to be rooted and grounded in penitence. Mercifully we can be pretty sure that the common life will bring us down in lowliness sooner or later, and when we remember that we have been set apart and spared the responsibilities of other ways of life in order to pursue the work of prayer, and that fundamentally it is here we shall be called to account, any corporate complacency ought soon to fade away.

21 March   The moment of glory is when God goes into the night of the utmost experience of dereliction…God is Love which knows in personal experience the farthest limits of un-love.

22 March   To follow Christ in love means not merely the observance of prohibitions and restrictions which we tend to associate with duty, but a glorious expansion into increasing awareness of the wholeness of his dwelling within our lives.

23 March   We limit the majestic mystery of redemption if we think too narrowly of Christ's obedience to the Father by enduring crucifixion and painful death. Rather, we should see in this great, living, ever-new event, the 'obedience' of God himself, being true to the nature of his love.

24 March   The conflict of light and darkness is basic in the mythology of many creeds and cultures: almost instinctively we expect and desire a conclusive outcome; and because 'Light' equals 'Right' we assume that it will eliminate the darkness. But the message of the Incarnation, the supreme saving action of God, is not that he has mightily overcome by superior force all that opposes his goodness and love; rather, that he has reversed our ideas of the manifestation and exercise of power and challenges us to accept the discomfort of sharing in the contest on his terms.

25 March   I love to be enfolded in Julian of Norwich and somehow permeated, as in a bubble bath, by her delight in the love of God and her everyday common sense approach.

26 March   Knowing that, as W. H. Vanstone says, nothing is outside the compass of the love of God we can be ready to share to the utmost man's alienation from God, if and as he permits us to do so, because Jesus himself is always there first, at the furthest point of desolation. Although by the nature of the case, we cannot know or feel benefit from this grace, no one's despair, our own or other people's, is ultimate or absolute.

27 March   I do thank God for you – hope *you* do, sometimes!

28 March   I think it's important that you…don't keep looking and hoping for 'growth' in the obvious, recognizable ways, and feeling regretful and panicky when it doesn't come like that…You must joyfully receive the is-ness of your successive present moments and respond to the opportunities they offer.

29 March I expect most of you feel, as I do myself, that one is really a fish out of water in a situation that does not provide the minimum framework of prayer ordered to punctuate the day and the night, and an acceptance of solitude and silence that enables one to live the whole of life spread out before God.

30 March Whatever the particular personal conditions of our life, we shall find in it accusingly empty spaces. Even the closest companionship leaves gaps, and the God who made us for himself is not always there to fill them.

Christians can make sense of the loneliness which is for so many people something terrifying to be avoided at all costs. If we walk towards it, into the wilderness, our perspective alters, and we discover new and unexpected richness in our situation when we can accept it as it is and stop regretting that it is not otherwise.

The spiritual wilderness does flower, and it is, as the early Fathers discovered the geographical desert to be, a lovable place if we are alert and expectant to search for and respond to all that is in it. All sorts of sudden delights will surprise us into wonder and loving worship.

31 March I used to make lists of 'current woes', and then had to make parallel ones of 'current unexpected blessings', because there were always those too.

1 April The image of Christ as clown…is appropriate because the clown is one who plays a tragic role without ever taking himself or life too seriously…(H)e can laugh at himself because he is devoid of conceit and self-importance, and radiates what has been well described as a 'childlike, unmalicious, frolicsome quality'.

2 April I think 'life' just *is* crazy for everyone. It certainly seems to be for everyone here!

3 April If we pray to have the mind of Christ, we must be ready to live by such a love that "in all things and above all things" goes out to God – not as we think or hope he may be, but as he knows he is: and that finds its justification and fulfilment not in any sense of certainty, but in the fact that it is called into being by his love for us.

4 April I think we have to take the consequences of giving people the freedom to be themselves, warts, mistakes, and all, and letting the hurt hurt, because that is probably God's way in.

5 April Health and fulness of life tend eventually to deterioration and decay, and many lives and personalities seem to have not even a chance of fulfilment. But Christian teaching is that "we do not lose heart. Though our outer nature is wasting away, our inner nature is being renewed every day" (2 Corinthians 4.16).

Renewal – that is one of the reasons why we pray. Through the example of the Cross we know that true life does indeed continue through death for the preservation of every link of love.

6 April Often we fail to hear one another because we are too afraid or preoccupied to listen openly: we fear the loss of something precious to ourselves, or we are too reluctant to risk the impingement upon us of another self if it comes too close.

But no one, however locked in loneliness by some particular anguish of body, mind, or spirit, is separated from the God who died 'outside the gate' in the extremity of God-forsakenness, and by doing so took the whole of creation into his unbroken unity. Although we feel we cannot be heard when we say this to someone in need, any more than we can hear it ourselves when we would wish to do so, we can trust God to make it known in ways beyond our reach; and we can believe, affirm, and live by the great and saving truth that he is Man and gives meaning to our existence.

7 April Now I am looking out on sunny Sussex countryside, having had a lovely, lazy, yet-more-holiday time here. It seems somewhat obscene to be so idle, but nevertheless I manage it very well.

8 April It is the Incarnation that redeems us all and gathers the whole of creation to God in Christ. So the 'good news' is not that Jesus as perfect man was killed to appease an angry God, but that God has lived a totally human life, including death, and so affirmed the eternal value of the cosmos and all that is in it.

9 April The conditions in which we live are artificial: a structured discipline (and a stringent one where it impedes our independence as regards use of time) enables us to carry out our profession of prayer, liturgical and personal. Deprivation of what is reckoned as a normal amount of culture and conversation (in the widest sense of that word), also of opportunity of outward ministry to the needs of others, drives us inwards and downwards in order that ultimately we can, by the grace of God, rise upwards and outwards, lifting our humanity to him in an offering made on behalf of all creation. But first we have to plumb self-awareness and those dangerous areas of illusion where everything gets out of proportion, imagination and memory run riot, and a sense of alienation from God, one another, and our own selves threatens to wreck us.

10 April I know I personally can never trust my own motives for doing anything – but so what? The object of our discipleship is not to 'do the right' (and so win credit in our own eyes) but to love God. I have found that I have just bumbled along through life, doing the next thing that turned up to be done, assuming that where there was a choice my motives were murky, and that my capacity for self-deception is infinite, but knowing that God knows more about all that than I do. (And while I understand all too well the niggling sense that 'the hardest thing is most pleasing to God', I know *that* must be downed at all costs!)

11 April Insofar as a religious community contains persons varying greatly in origin, social status, training, and tastes, it represents a cross-section of human society, and its responsibility to transcend differences to a degree beyond mutual toleration and peaceful coexistence is a solemn one. The radical organization of our baptismal promises in religious profession cannot increase our commitment to God, which is already total, but it does underline it by a conscious, responsible decision, made not out of duty or for pleasure, but to affirm the folly of faith.

12 April I believe that the 'white martyrs' as well as the others must be prepared, to quote Eberhard Bethge's biography of Dietrich Bonhoeffer, to "undergo the agony of universal rejection...physical and psychological isolation...without any attempt at justification..." We have to be stripped of all delusions and preconceived ideas about ourselves and one another if our humanity is to be able to grow to its true glory in freedom from fear, and this process is painful and slow. The important thing above all is that we can never have a God's eye view of things. Do not let us get bogged down in all we can see of the immediate present concerns, and lose the overall, wider perspective. This means a lack of intense preoccupation, a certain 'sitting lightly' to life which in no way diminishes the high seriousness and urgency with which we regard our vocation – but not, I hope, ourselves. Let us keep a sense of proportion, and, if possible, of humour.

13 April ...we must inevitably experience in close and costly consciousness the impingement upon us of those with whom we are involved whether through intercessory prayer or in direct contact. We do not have to stand up and be counted, risking obloquy and humiliation as pacifists and antinuclear arms protesters; we do not have to make decisions and declare ourselves in respect of the major controversial issues of our day. In most cases we do not have enough information to justify our doing so anyway. But unless we are expecting to live more comfortably, less compromisedly, and less committedly than we should outside the Community, we must be prepared to be exposed to an awareness of the contemporary situation based on the knowledge of the roots of human sin in our own hearts: sin that is recognized, repented of, and, in the mercy of God, forgiven and redeemed through Love.

14 April   God's loving care for each sparrow of us doesn't save us from the horrors and hazards of created life, but accompanies us in it all. And intercession is believing in, and abiding by, and affirming *that*.

15 April   I believe that if we are called to a life of prayer lived in community, it is in order that we may be exposed to all the facets of interior life that one would like to avoid and that are inevitably obscured if our concern is with a ministry that is primarily one of thinking and doing. In so far as this Community is called – and it is, individually and corporately – to such ministry, that is secondary to the basic spiritual experience of being spread out before God, in prayed life, for the sake of the world. We give ourselves to be available to know personally, if and as God wills, the whole range of human experience, good and bad: fears, fantasies, loneliness and confusion, the sense of separation from God, but also of union with Him…This, I think, is what a life's work of prayer is about: and yet sometimes it seems that 'prayer' is regarded by Christians as a relieved relinquishing of one's worries into the hands of a benevolent Deity who will 'make all well' on our terms.

16 April   [Written in 1991 and after commenting on the Gulf War] It's essential, isn't it, to realize that God does not see things as we do, and our business is to do what we can, when we can, in our own small sphere. We are to let the agony of others impinge on us, but not to get emotionally involved, which doesn't help them. Actually, the only way to do *that* is to give ourselves to God, isn't it? I think that's the only way to convey his love to others, too. Trying to talk about it in a way that they will understand doesn't seem to work. But trying to be loving, to God and to people, does – except that this happens in ways we don't expect. As you say, it's 'caught', not 'taught'.

17 April   A great danger in our life is that of introspection and self-absorption. It is vitally important that our prayer life with God should be based on a reality of relationship with other people. If we don't stand back from others enough to see them as they really are

– and give them room to be themselves – the chances are that in our prayer we shall be projecting our own image on to God and worshipping that. Contact and communication are essential to prevent the fantasies that so easily grow up in isolation when things get out of all proportion. We need to submit ourselves to the impact of one another's personalities, and here the common intention is vitally important, because if we concentrate on glorifying *God* through relationships, they won't become ends in themselves with the stronger in danger of dominating, and the weaker becoming aggressive in self-defence.

18 April [A Rogation Eucharist] Seeing the consecrated bread (an entire roll) passed round and consumed – all gone, because in us! So we *are* the Body of Christ.

19 April All we need to fear is our own blindness, and if we really put our trust in God we can be happily ready for anything and surprised by nothing. But he will always demand more of us than we think we have got to give, for to aim at perfection and perpetually to fall short is the great tradition of monastic life since the days of the desert fathers (and mothers).

20 April When physically I can't *do* anything Godward, when emotionally I can't *feel* anything Godward, when intellectually I can't *believe* anything Godward, I seem to get more firmly convinced that God is who and how I'd most hope.

21 April I remember at one point in my Fairacres non-career writing a letter to God from the depths of Sheol and finding that I *was* thankful for the hopelessness and humiliation because when one had lost *everything* then there was no more stripping to be done.

22 April If we trust the goodwill Godwards of our sisters, we may risk betrayal, as God does, but we shall be...glimpsing the reflection of God in one another and finding something of the infinite potential of true selves, our own and our sisters'. Can we accept the 'odd things' other people do, and also their questioning and sometimes disapproval of what we ourselves do? Such acceptance transcends safety, security, and common sense. If it is contained in the Love of God, it can, as Father Peter Allen said in a homily at Fairacres on Ascension Day, "awaken deep trust in others, trust which will overcome that deep distrust between nations, between races, between families that is the deep, deep concern of our prayer."

23 April   I now listen to the Gospels rather than reading them and I am struck by many new insights, not least how enigmatic and ambiguous are many of Jesus' sayings and doings. He is essentially paradoxical and reveals God as just that. And because it's beyond our grasp we don't like it and we want to get him taped and packaged.

24 April   [On rashness, the desire to take short cuts, impatience, self-choosings] We have to combat this by learning to accept the long slow plodding way that is the only safe one – and the fact that there is often no substitute for time. God will not allow us the satisfaction of shedding our faults directly we are aware of them: we will have to learn that we are part of the whole lump of sin, and to experience the consequences of this in terms of situations inside and outside ourselves that just have to be accepted and lived through because they are not such as can be 'put right'. Perhaps we are experiencing this...when we meet at close quarters men and women of other races, colours, and creeds, and can share painfully in the effects of sin and disunity by having to know realistically what they suffer without being able to remedy the situation.

25 April   ...I accept the 'right' co-existence of contradictions because I recognize a dimension beyond my comprehension. But while acknowledging that love is indefinable, I can abide in the ultimate 'All shall be well'. But the way there is pretty grotty for such as you, I fear.

26 April When 'God' is no longer received through liturgy, common life, and observance, the essence of him and his love and fun comes bubbling out of very mundane, secular sources, and even the awfulness doesn't manage to have quite the last word.

27 April "For others and for ourselves": the purpose of our existence is something – or Someone – beyond what we actually do. Personally we probably experience the discipline of the timetable as constricting and frustrating, constantly thwarting our completion of what we want to do, be this 'work' or 'leisure' activity, when and how we want to do it. But, of course, we have freely chosen to devote our lives to giving God priority, and this is what the common life enables us to do. If that is compromised, then the various outward and visible expressions of our prayer, whether personal or corporate, are inappropriate.

28 April I do agree about the motherhood of God, and I think that...'passive' (not flabby) receptivity is part of it. The Father God figure incites to 'telling people what' and 'putting things right'. But Jesus' way of accepting the painful results of people's trying to find their own way rings true. I think that is the feminine aspect of God. I believe women's ministry in the Church is to practise this (rather than preach it, which is again a very masculine activity)...I don't think it is the way forward for women to become female male-priests, but that once they are ordained the ballyhoo will run out of steam.

29 April Whether or not we personally 'enjoy' discussions, I think they are forming in us a disposition of openness and exposure – readiness to listen to other people and fearlessly to state our own views – which can draw us together at a point slightly beyond anyone's 'prepared position'. The fact of being able to meet one another better is more important than what is actually said (though of course everyone's contribution is valuable and worthwhile) and helps to create a corporate frame of mind in which we can hear and respond to God. I believe we are being drawn down into a depth of receptivity where we can together learn more about reconciliation than we have known before. This does not mean reaching agreement or even consensus: it means glimpsing the essence of that which is divisive – in any situation, not only ours – and learning to contain it because we know that it is held and transfigured in the crucified and risen Redeemer. I think that we are only beginning to be taught of God about this, and it is vital that we do our learning corporately.

30 April   I don't think it's any use trying to make oneself feel safe about dying: better to face squarely the fact that at gut level one's scared stiff sometimes and to learn to live with that…I used to think that a 'strong faith' would be a safeguard against fearing death, but I don't any more.

1 May   I am sure that the deepest desire of each one of us is sound and sincere, and we must not pay too much attention to the superficial froth and ferment of inter-reaction among us in respect of which the passage of time usually restores a right sense of proportion. Nor must we diminish one another and our own selves by our expectations or by our interpretations of what we see and understand, but take care always to be thoroughly affirmative and to believe the best.

2 May   I do find that being incapacitated brings out the best of human kindness everywhere, and I am so grateful.

3 May   I suppose that 'praying constantly' means coming more and more to know and accept the impossibility of making sense of the way things are. I know we must do what we can for social justice and the other cardinal virtues, but ultimately we have to depend on the gift of God's grace in order to believe beyond sight in his way of love.

4 May   Father Staniloae says: "Christianity has revealed the aptitude of every human being for holiness, and the aptitude of the
whole world for reflecting that holiness." It is our life's work to
affirm this great truth, and to witness to the fact that God's dimension includes and transcends that of the lovely but suffering everyday world. To take, as his children, our appointed part in his work
of redemption means not so much trying to eliminate sin, evil, and
suffering, but regarding them from a perspective whence it can be
seen that the love of God transmutes them into good. Even in our
own little lives we so often see pain and unhappiness – ours and
other people's – as sheerly bad; consequently, we can get worked up
and distressed to the extent of missing the opportunity to lay the
situation before God and let him into it.

5 May   If an association between persons is to be real, demanding,
and supportive, beyond belonging to a friendly club of like-minded
people, there's got to be some sort and degree of costly commitment – to each according to his need, from each according to his
ability. And the understanding of that and willingness to play along
is needful, isn't it, from the outset? A readiness to put *oneself* in the
pot, so to speak. Not just one's ideas, theories, suggestions, from
which one can distance oneself, but the tender, skinless part!

6 May   Prayer is not a monologue. If it is a matter of communication we must be listening to God in our hearts, to one another,
and to the rest of creation all the time; and we should be ready to
let go of our own desires, expectations, and preconceived ideas.
It is a help to remember that communication, whether or not it is
regarded as part of prayer, can never be wholly successful. How
often we are misunderstood, misrepresented, and amazed that
others can see something so completely differently from the way
we do. Yet unless there has been deliberate falsification, the
chances are that both points of view, however apparently contra-
dictory in our limited apprehension, are parts of the truth of the
matter. Only God knows the whole of any person or situation.

7 May   I was genuinely smitten the other day when the scripture reading was from Proverbs 6.6: "Go to the ant thou sluggard." However, I ignored it, and I find 'letting go' becomes more and more pleasant and possible the more one perfects the art.

8 May   I hate the idea of reincarnation! It feels like going backwards to have more than one life. I'd like to think of perpetual progress. But, as you say, there are many stranger things in heaven and earth that we wot not of.

9 May   When I get the impact of the godlessness of the world through radio and tapes, I can't be smug and godly, but in the same lostness, helplessness, and apparent godlessness myself. I think that's the way Jesus intercedes for us, by being alongside and not other.

10 May   …while it may be right for one or two (not always the same one or two) to make journeys and to give instruction, backed by the prayer and acceptance of the Community as a whole, the Sisters of the Love of God are basically called to folly and hiddenness, to giving ourselves in darkness, ignorance, and bewilderment to God, so that he can work through us more than we could ever imagine for the welfare of the world. Only if undertaken against this background can our departures from 'ordinary life' be justified. But I do believe that on occasion they are not only justified but demanded. Our stability is of purpose, not of place; our wilderness is a way of life that fosters in each of us a reality of response to God that should inevitably incur risk-taking…Exclusive and continuous attention to God is grounded not so much on physical separation from the world as on a dynamic personal relationship to him to which all Christians are called…

11 May   Alas, pressure groups in parishes can be very distressing, for the incumbent and other parishioners. I suppose you just have to meet each situation as it comes, relying – as you say – on prayer, and not to have too many preconceived ideas. But you have found already in your ministry that *listening*, and a readiness to change one's mind, are essential pastorally. I'm glad you intend to be firm about ensuring *time* away from practical parochial activities. After all, your chief work for God through your people (a rather old-fashioned expression, I fear!) is *being* rather than *doing*, isn't it?

12 May   I do reiterate my conviction that you are doing right to go headlong *into* the difficulty of dissension at home. You will always be alongside the Crucified Lord and used by him to effect transfiguration and reconciliation not only in your community but in the world at large. Whether or not we see results is immaterial.

13 May   I think the Church is all wrong when it puts lids on doctrine. In St John's discourses (John 12–17) I'm hearing Jesus say that he's got much to say which they (and we) can't hear yet, but that the Holy Spirit will lead us into all truth. Of course, it's a risky way and we can't just hare off after any old whim; but, equally, we can't get stuck. I think the fact that it *is* his Body keeps the Church going somehow, and that although ninety-nine per cent of it (us) is wrong in one way or another, there's still a one per cent at the core that keeps it lurching on.

14 May   It is imperative to recognize and retain our human ignorance and powerlessness if we are truly to appreciate the dignity bestowed upon us by God's love and grace. That, in ourselves and in others, we ignore at our peril.

15 May   Always it's a question of accepting terms other than one's own, isn't it, and one (this one, anyway!) is so well able to assume that one's own terms are synonymous with God's.

16 May   Someone said recently, "Well, *I* can't see what God can make of this mess." To which the answer was, "Well it doesn't matter two pins that you can't understand." I find that when I'm fretting about something, if my mind can tell my emotions, "Well, there it is, you can't un-happen it, so get on with it," they take their course. In the passage of time the fret dies out and we see that what has distressed us doesn't matter objectively all that much, and that there are other things that are much more important. In the case of something major like your accident, the working through of the emotional and physical distress will take some time, and it can't, and shouldn't, be hurried. But if your spirit can get detached quickly, that helps a lot.

17 May   Christians are being asked by God to look quite afresh at sexuality in its *widest* sense. I'm sure we've got to get right away from cultural taboos and see in the light of the Gospel that *if*, as Christians we say Yes to discipline and the way of the Cross, then as persons we must face and come to terms with our sexuality, and give free rein to our affections because we shall be able to say No when appropriate, and to accept the pain of non-fulfilment physic-ally, which God can and will transfigure into something very rich and good for the whole purpose of salvation.

18 May   Our goal is fellowship with God, which is not something static, but dynamic. Being with him is to keep on exploring and becoming. Death is an incident on the journey. It is to be with him in his work of drawing all things into unity and love. This together-ness with God depends entirely on his love. We can't earn it or safe-guard it. Trust it even when it feels not to be there. Go with him into the unexpected, the frightening, the altogether unknown and pray that he will have mercy on the world.

19 May   God knows better than we do what wretched sinners we are: so we do not have to go on telling him. He knows that we owe everything to him, and he wants from us not grovelling gratitude but lifelong companionship.

20 May   There are so many ways, recognized and unrecognized, in which we try to turn away from what is being offered and asked through circumstances. But it is probably just when we are feeling most exposed, with raw edges smarting, unable to escape or with-draw because of those nailing vows, that God turns to speak to us, where we are, in community. Quite often, if we are wholly there when he turns to speak to us, we hear that our current difficulty – whether due to circumstances or to personalities – is to be neither resolved nor removed, but lived with.

21 May   We may think, and rightly, that we have been called into the wilderness to be a sign to the Church and to the world, but we know all too well how dangerously easy it is to miss what has been called 'the narrow way of Jesus' even there.

22 May   ...we can't believe that the whole of humankind has to join the Christian Church. God is much larger than that. We've got to do what is to hand in our own sphere and not try and organize everyone else according to our own ideas of what God wants.

23 May   Are we willing to feel skinned, afraid and isolated, and to say a Gethsemane Yes with Jesus to life – and death – as they come to us? Therein is the reality of obedience.

24 May   I think I told you that for me 'prayer' – being still, in hope, before God – as I used to know it has just *gone*. But God, bless him, hasn't. Even when I don't 'believe' in him, this makes sense because I think the message of the Incarnation is that God is in *every* aspect of the human condition and now incarnate in living Christians, and, as my beloved Moltmann says in *The Crucified God*, "No one can be further from God than God has himself been."

25 May   If we believe we are called to give our lives to God in and through this Community we gladly accept that it will cost everything; but it is only as time goes on that the implications of what that involves are borne in upon us. Inch by inch we are stripped of what we did not know that we possessed. Poverty is experienced not in terms of material deprivation so much as in the whittling away of our image of ourselves. This happens in many and varied ways, and can be devastating. Yet destitution, spiritual as well as temporal, is a great leveller. We know that when God deals with us in his own inimitable way, 'in community', we are indeed all in the same boat. Perhaps the most important thing we do as a family is mutually to contain one another. We know we are accepted when we are found to be nothing but our basic selves, as we accept others in the same state; and although sometimes we experience and cause exasperation, fundamentally we cannot make value judgments about one another. We can only stand before God to say 'Kyrie eleison' from the depths of our own hearts on behalf of ourselves, our Community, and the world we represent.

26 May ...there is nothing static about living in the wilderness close to God, it is intensely dynamic. If our vows 'crucify us', it is in the sense that our wilfulness and independence are brought up short against the fact that we have freely chosen to submit them to the Community, and by that means to hand them over to God. But we are not concerned primarily with being dead, but with living anew in Christ.

27 May Yes, I'm sure it's so important to realize that *God's love for us* is what matters supremely, and that *that* is the last word, not all the dreariness and despondency that get on top of us. Nor are our efforts necessary or effective! Humbling indeed: but perhaps it's a thought that can help us towards a truer perspective.

28 May On lifelong commitment: the way into the open heart surgery that, in my opinion, sheds the love of God abroad in the world, as Jesus did.

29 May And poverty: Somebody said to me recently that material wealth can insulate one from hardship, which led me to think that although we have willy-nilly security and physical well-being, we may not possess or appropriate for ourselves anything we do as members of the Community. We each have to take responsibility for knowing and being the people we are, to place our own self willingly into the 'common stock', and receive from there the reality of the other selves who are our sisters.

30 May   Coming back to 'waiting', I persist in believing that "the faith and the hope and the love are all in the waiting", as Eliot says. I think that a sense of God and a sense of prayer have to be let go of, and even, maybe, the conviction that he *is*, so that we live with risk, and the possibility of self-delusion.

31 May   My 'mantra' is: "All of You, nothing of me", and Father Gilbert gave it to me when I was wondering how to talk to novices when I was feeling helpless about becoming Novice Mistress. Somehow it has remained as a guiding principle and is a help in trying to say Yes underneath things, when that is the answer which seems to be required. I think God always leaves us with a choice, and we *could* say No. So we don't even have the assurance that he'll keep us pointed rightly in spite of ourselves.

1 June   When I stopped being Mother, God gave me a sort of 'golden handshake'. Suddenly everything appeared in a new perspective: the 'affairs of state' which, miniscule though they be, had filled my horizon for so long, took their rightful subordinate place besides the work of God, which I mean not just us in Choir, but *God's* use of our lives (and all lives, not only Christian or monastic ones). And there was a quiet unwonted conviction that in a 'beyond' place, in God, all *is* well. I am so grateful for that glimpse, way beyond 'desire' even, let alone 'desert'. I think that ordinarily we have to experience personally the anguish and woe of the world, both what happens to us and what happens to others, so that the impingement of it is real. But always we have to believe that the last word is with love. And that love is not only *beyond*, but *through* pain, for God as well as for us…It's impossible to comprehend, barely to apprehend. But somehow I think we have to hold together the contradictions in tension so that while we lament the awfulness of everything, and our contribution thereto, we rejoice in the marvel of God and his love.

2 June   …the expectations and assumptions of those among whom you minister are inevitably 'of the world'. Certainly we are wracked here with competitiveness, envy, jealousy, and all uncharitableness. But we can see them for what they are. But in a parish there will automatically be pressure to 'increase numbers' etc., to produce results which show. The truth is that a congregation of one can exercise an infinite apostolate through prayer lived.

3 June   Which of us could claim that she has 'grown up'? I know I could not. But that does not matter, as long as we know where we are, why we are there, and how we are to grow onwards.

4 June   The way of self-discovery is often one of eruptions and explosions if we are prepared to face our human problems as and where they are rather than to escape by spiritualizing them. Everyone, while finding that to come to terms with other people is a way to do so with herself, must be prepared to do her share of, so to speak, 'containing nuclear waste' for the common good.

5 June   How terrifying evil is, and one feels so helpless. It is frightening when there is nothing left to hold on to except the head knowledge that Love in Christ *has* overcome, not in *victory* but in *defeat*. But when in the face of so much suffering in the world one feels defeated, *ipso facto* the head knowledge doesn't cut much ice.

6 June   Jesus was hungry, thirsty, tired, according to the Gospels. Presumably he was also sometimes irritated and impatient, found life as untidy and full of dilemmas as we do, had to make, not clear-cut decisions between black and white, but bewildering ones between different, or sometimes identical, shades of grey. Probably he made mistakes and wrong judgments – though who is to say, in most cases, what ultimately proves to be 'wrong'? Surely we cannot claim that the sinless Jesus had a complacent sense of his own virtue, for St Paul says he was 'made to be sin', which seems to imply an experience of the self-disgust and hopelessness which most of us know at some time or another.

All through this typically human experience, Jesus lived in a spirit of self-giving love towards God and man which brought on him the death through which sin and evil have been finally conquered. The 'hard and bitter agony' which the Incarnation means for us, is to choose in our own lives to live in the same spirit of self-giving love which, though it cuts across our natural inclinations, is possible because we belong to him.

7 June I believe that anxiety is largely due to lack of a true perspective. Things loom so large and are so devastating, in anticipation or in memory – seldom in actuality, oddly enough – because I attach a disproportionate importance to my being humiliated. In the course of a fairly long life I've got quite used to that happening, and I realize too that people are not going to spend half as much time thinking about me negatively as I assume they will, and so I am better able to take it all in the day's work. I think too that it's important to take account of the temperament with which each of us is endowed. If that is an anxious one, well, it's part of the tools we've got to work with, and it is pointless to wish to refashion oneself, and undesirable. Acceptance of and coming to terms with me-as-I-am can make for peace of mind.

8 June Exacted from us is an attitude to earthly life, living each moment to the full, which is a proclamation that the kingdom of heaven is here and now if only we have eyes to see.

9 June We cannot attempt to justify God's ways, or presume to think we know what he should do; but we can affirm our faith and hope and love by willingly 'keeping on keeping on' in the face of life's impasses, and by being alert to delight in the evidences of God's love and care which are there for eyes that can see them. And we can try always to offer the whole gamut of human experience to God, trusting him to use us for his purposes, which are beyond our understanding.

10 June   I do not think a really God-centred love can be diminished by expansion; and mercifully the use he makes of us does not depend upon our command of charm and affability.

11 June   John Donne, nearly four centuries ago, in his poem 'Satyre III', wrote:

> To stand inquiring right, is not to stray;
> To sleep or run wrong, is. On a huge hill,
> Cragged, and steep, Truth stands, and he that will
> Reach her, about must, and about must go.

It is becoming increasingly clear that unless we take seriously the message of these lines, the human race is in danger of destroying itself. We must surely recognize that no single person can rightly claim to be able to apprehend the 'whole' truth even if they believe it to be contained in their particular revealed religion.

As Christians knowing Truth as a Person, we realize that 'reaching her' involves an infinite journey into the infinite God. Nevertheless, he is our companion on the way as are also the myriad other mortals, past, present, and future, going 'about and about' up the 'huge hill' like ourselves, and catching all the time different facets from different angles of the one Truth.

12 June   In Christianity the primacy of self-interest and the outlook of 'reward and punishment' gradually gives place to an understanding of sacrificial love that is prepared to know 'the fellowship of his sufferings', so that there can be a universal resurrection from the dead.

13 June   …the challenge and opportunity to go beyond the 'It isn't fair' attitude to acceptance of apparent injustice where it hurts *me*.

14 June   It seems to me that God wants us to do more about living together in mutual *liking*, rather than dismissing…affection as something given or withheld by nature, and so being content to conclude that *loving* is all that matters…

Really to bother to know and understand another person will, with determination and goodwill, bring one eventually to discover that this is the stuff of which the Love of God is made. We can, alas, all too readily proclaim with Charlie Brown's friend Linus, that "we love mankind; it's human beings we can't stand."

15 June In uttering words of psalms and prayers we aren't so much asking for specific things as aligning ourselves with God that his will be done. "Thou shalt see thy desire upon thine enemies" means seeing them absorbed in his love and transfigured. (NB So many nuances spring to life in Coverdale's version that one returns to it after a variety of modern ones.)

16 June [On hearing of a death] Surely not according to the will of God, but equally not outside the compass of his love.

17 June Jesus teaches us to look at each individual person as unique and to consider the particular circumstances of every case in which a decision has to be made. This is not easy, but each of us can try in the limited sphere of our little lives not to be pressurized into mass thinking. Instead, we need to remember the friendly greetings, the words of encouragement and sympathy, the small acts of kindness which people exchange a thousand times a day, and most of all in times of trouble, and which are the true measure of the spirit of humankind.

18 June I think my term 'absorbing evil' is misleading. I totally agree with you that being too open and exposed to the horrific forces that are around can destroy the personality – though even then, in madness or suicide, I believe the *person* is held in the loving care of God. Those who are psychically sensitive help people to 'shut off' from evil when they encounter it in a way that seems comparable to what you call 'growing a thicker skin'.

If God uses us in the halting of evil it can be done only by *him* through us. It would be insufferably arrogant and dangerous to think we could do anything about it in our own strength.

19 June   I think the last thing God wants from us is submission made out of *fear*. And as I get older I find how large a part of my life is dominated by that, and what a key motive it is in so many actions.

20 June   I think...that stillness is a quality of spirit which can exist even without conditions of silence. Of course those help to get it established. But basically it is a question of acceptance and surrender to what *is*. Not easy.

21 June   The repudiation of the double standard means that far from seeing the religious life as a way where relationships are lived in a manner exemplary to the rest of Christendom, we know it as one which shows up quite remorselessly our basic self-centredness. "What is a weed, exactly?" asks John Stuart Collis in *The Worm Forgives the Plough*. "It is any plant which impedes or competes with any other particular plant we are interested in." How often do we see our sisters as weeds impeding us! A shocking question, perhaps, but let us be honest and agree that it needs to be asked.

22 June   It is not so much a question of clock time spent in silence and solitude as of an attitude of mind that gives priority to waiting on God only. We are all able to lock ourselves into solitude designed according to our own specifications, protected from intruders. But if we are truly trying to put God first, we shall gradually grow to find him, and trust him, in persons and things – but above them – and to find all persons and things in him.

23 June   ...the way forward is not the way of great schemes and preconceived plans...but the way of practical fidelity in the present moment: something incredibly easy to talk about, and impossibly difficult to carry out. But the 'dedication demands rejoicing' and we need not wait until the end of the world for that.

24 June   ...if we *can* let the darkness and emptiness 'come upon us', I believe they prove to be more friendly than we expect.

25 June   Evil is contagious. It can be contained and defeated, as Dr C.B. Caird writes in his commentary on the Beatitudes, "only when hatred, insult, and injury are absorbed and neutralized" by love…

Thanks to our belief that 'God is as he is in Jesus', we know that his love does absorb evil, and that we can ourselves be enabled to extend to others and to receive from them forgiveness in this way.

26 June   The clouded sense of loss, absence, and unknowing is as much prayer as are the moments of dazzling awareness.

27 June   We must certainly be ready to give and take as persons and to persevere through the difficulties this involves; but we have to remember that the Community is bigger than the sum of its members, and we can surely believe that there is an eschatological element in the encounters we have within it, and a depth and durability about these which depend on God and not on ourselves. This can be a consoling thought when we feel simply stumped, but it must never be made an excuse for giving up at the level where we can act.

28 June   "The love of Christ has joined us together." If we 'love' one another because of Christ it means that his mind is in us to a degree that makes us able to 'receive' one another as God does. We shall not necessarily find one another more congenial on a natural level; but we shall apprehend a little of the divine truth in our fellow human beings – and perhaps eventually even in ourselves. The element of 'letting go' is built into all our relationships by our vow of chastity, and we look for their fulfilment in our common convergence on God. We do not have to take too seriously the tiffs and traumas that sometimes fill our immediate horizon, but we do need to recognize these as part of the stuff of life and means of response to vocation. There is no situation in which we cannot pray 'God', and often when we know ourselves to be culpable and feel ashamed, as well as ill-tempered, we have got an opportunity that he can use.

29 June You're so right about interruptions. I am desperately stuck in my ways here, and very put out if my self-organized little routine is in any way disturbed by outside persons or factors. But I think one just has to accept that that's the way one is, and quite a large part of life's work is putting up with oneself. I am sure that growth in prayer means increasing willingness to be exposed to what happens and to accept whatever is, *as it is*, suffering the consequences – and, of course, enjoying to the full, and not wasting time on regrets.

30 June ...I realize how much of the Mother's function in our present situation of being one community in four houses is inevitably concerned with communication at a deeper level than simply exchange of information. Her business is not primarily with the practicalities of life which plenty of other sisters are well equipped to cope with. Her job is to be equally available to every sister in the terms required by our Rule, and she cannot, while she holds the office, meet her sisters in a peer relationship. The sister/mother one is part of reality, and there is no point in regretting that one cannot have everything at once. 'Mother' just has to remember that she does not see sisters as they see one another, nor does she know herself as they know her. It is important for her and everyone else to accept that she is not omniscient any more than she is omnipotent, but perhaps by the virtue of her office and role she has a view of situations that makes a necessary contribution to the Community's understanding of them. And she has reason more than anyone else to believe that things do evolve, that people do grow in the Spirit, and that miracles do happen: whatever the difficulty, if we stay with it and let the hurt hurt, in the end something shifts.

✣

1 July [On different expressions of our common vocation]: ... anything that any of us does is common property, not our own 'thing'. It has to be submitted and shared by the sister concerned, and received and cared about by the rest of us. In this way there can grow a unity of responsibility that is fuller and deeper than the uniformity which many of us used to regard as the *sine qua non* of religious life.

2 July ...with God silence is essentially a positive thing. We receive it as negative when he is not communicating as we want, when we want. I've been thinking a lot about the need and desire to articulate things as a bid for control.

3 July [After a meeting with one of the many people who knew Sister Jane as a 'soul friend'] I spent Night Office feeling like Balaam's ass. I'm sure if God gets anything across to you through your visits here, it's in spite of, not because of the parlour maid who serves the boiled cabbage or cold beetroot! But I suppose if God's got any reason for putting you in the way of Balaam's ass, that creature must bray as it can.

4 July Obviously you must...hold on to the still centre in your personal, parochial, and political life, all of which are inextricably mixed; and from our side, with such a centre apparently secured by our protected and privileged conditions, we find that in our little lives we experience very vividly the consequences of living in what we are praying about! So perhaps a 'common cause' of minding most about the dimension of life eternal can bridge the gap between us in life temporal.

5 July It probably seems and is presumptuous, but I do believe your terrible breakdown experience was, and is, redemptive. At a perceptible level there was the sheer courage of clawing your way back to life, and there is also the undeniable enrichment it must have brought to your work. But there is more, on a spiritual level, that cannot be articulated.

6 July   Watching and fasting demonstrate a mild defiance of natural rhythms in order to emphasize the prior importance of God's dimension.

7 July   ...how important a part of our vocation is the work of old age. It is true that in community we are given care and security denied to many; but it is also true that nothing alleviates the particular loneliness experienced as our faculties diminish and our independence is stripped away. We who are still active and functionally responsible know the loving power that there is in the prayed lives of our senior sisters, but I doubt if you in that category recognize it yourselves. I think that true obedience, in terms of the 'Yes to the inevitable' wrung out of Jesus in Gethsemane, lies in quiet consent to an existence that has become or is becoming incapacitated, and this is what we are asked to practise...

8 July   One of my sisters carves little crosses to be held in the hand. She said she would show me the process of completing one, and when she brought it in the first stage, the rough shape hewn out of the block of wood, I thought, "She hasn't made it, she's discovered what's always there." And I followed this through: the cross at the heart of creation, "the Lamb slain from the foundation of the world" (Revelation 13.8).

9 July   ...we do not regard the common life as a necessary evil to be endured for the sake of a way of living wholly directed Godward, nor as a safe nesting place among like-minded people. Commitment to God in community through the vows is the means by which we are nailed to the cross of our order. At times we may be crucified by loneliness or by proximity: either way it is, as Father Gilbert Shaw so often reminded us, a bloody business and not to be lightly undertaken. But if we look into St Irenaeus' words in the context of the professed life, we shall see that through it we glorify God by being wholly and vibrantly human – and that this comes about when our gaze is fixed firmly on God.

10 July   What we do within the whole context of the Community's understanding of the contemplative life is relatively unimportant: why and how we do it matter supremely.

11 July   Humour is near to holiness, and love to laughter. That is why seemingly desperate situations in personal relationships or international affairs – for world politics depend ultimately on encounters between individuals – can often be resolved if the people concerned can simply smile at one another.

12 July   Our point of unity is in God. And although we may be required to experience within ourselves and among ourselves the essence of the estrangement that is racking the world now, as it has done throughout recorded time, we know that this exposure to the forces of conflict, this searing doubt, this seeming to fall through the bottom of all that was certain, can be survived, because we are among those with whom we are fundamentally and totally in accord at the point of ultimate commitment to God.

13 July   Because God shares our life, we share his, and physical death is a question of change, not extinction. But this in no way minimises the pain caused by parting from beloved persons or places. Nor does conviction about spiritual togetherness alleviate the anguish of actual apartness.

To grieve realistically about the one is not to deny the other. Thoroughly to accept loss without trying selfishly to hold on to the departed can, in fact, lead the bereaved forward to a liberation and some comprehension of what is beyond. It is, however, easier to speculate about this in theory than to believe it in the midst of experience.

Death belongs with time: it ends our portion of it. But death does not, cannot, erase the love that lived within the time of our lives, for love is greater than death and ascends with our souls into life eternal.

14 July Christians, in or outside the religious life, can all too easily become grim, tight-lipped practitioners of self-sacrifice. We concentrate far more on ourselves and the offering we heroically make than on God. If we really love him everything will be freely and gladly given, regardless of what we feel in terms of consolations or awareness of him. We can shrivel into empty shells if we allow ourselves to be enslaved by duty, devoting ourselves entirely to the impossible task of trying to fulfil, to our own satisfaction, the exigencies of a particular role we may happen to occupy at the time.

15 July And if we really hand over to God we risk being 'unedifying' by dying in fear and without faith, because that ultimately is his problem and the fact that my pride suffers is immaterial.

16 July [On the importance of the praying] Sheer plonk, and *staying with it*, in God's broken heart, if that doesn't sound mawkish. Even if it does, in fact, because I must try, if I am to be of any use for you in God's dealings with you, to say what seems to me to be true, and just hope for the best. And I don't really care about 'my image' in your view!

17 July If we really live what we say, our witness should be a glorious affirmation that physical death is something in parenthesis and that the dimension entered into by contemplative life and prayer (not the exclusive prerogative of enclosed communities) is one which can be known as continuous, either side of that formidable barrier.

18 July We know well that each person is an unpredictable and unfathomable mystery: unique, incomparable, and with a purpose in life that only he or she can fulfil. If we manage to believe this about ourselves and one another in community we must remember that those attributes of personhood apply supremely to what little we can know of who God is, and that he is dynamic and unexpected in his treatment of us all. However, in our particular expression of

Christian living we believe that we are here together because of one another's 'reciprocal love' for God, so that in all aspects of our common life we need to be looking beyond the immediate situation towards him. Solutions to problems will not be found in 'confronting' one another or any particular circumstances, but in our own endeavour to aim Godwards and our trust that others involved are trying to do the same.

19 July   Are we prepared to risk the exigencies of chastity by allowing ourselves to love and be loved in the context of a letting-go that is built in from the start because of the sheer fact that we belong to God by pledge? Paradoxically, this vow exposes us to closer human relationships than many of us would wish for or find comfortable.

20 July   Here, surely, is something for us to grasp and affirm: God, partaking of human nature and subject to its badness and goodness, which is still what it has always been, has made a statement about the ultimate defeat of hatred and evil. Love prevails.

21 July   Testing times teach one compassion, an ability to help others in a way nothing else does. The rule of prayer of a little Lutheran community in Hamburg…says: "If any situation cannot be made into prayer, the fault is not in the situation, but in ourselves." Horribly true, but not easy to act on, I find.

22 July   …inward, as well as, perhaps, our outward, silence would be more real and tranquil if we improved our communications… sometimes a deal of inward questionings and wonderment could be saved by simple knowledge of facts.

23 July   More and more I find it impossible to articulate anything coherent and intelligible about God! I'm always thankful that I personally am not required to preach and teach: but of course you *are*. I think it's generally true that if one speaks to others about God out of one's own experience – even if that is of bewilderment and unknowing – that carries conviction…By the end of my time as

Mother I was sufficiently carefree not to mind making a mess of
things at Chapter, and to be seen to be at a loss, and to stay silent,
trying first to pray my usual rhythm prayer, until there seemed to
be something real I could say...I think that having the humility to
know not only that we don't know, but also that we can't know, is
something important for the human race to learn.

24 July   In the life of prayer, intercession is for many of us...the
purpose of the whole of life. No human being can escape the fact
that we are all inextricably involved with our fellows – and with the
whole of creation. We are not only affected by one another's
actions but share the same basic human nature and cannot avoid
taking account of one another, simply because we have to inhabit
the same globe.

   Intercession is the basis of any attempt to find a *modus vivendi* and
to look beyond the confrontation of conflicting interests to convergence in a common good.

25 July   The ultimate purpose of...Christ's Body, the Church, is not
to live in hearty fellowship, doing good to others. It is so to have in
and amongst us the mind of Christ, the spirit of his sacrificial love,
that as we live, profoundly sharing and caring in the world, we meet
the assaults and effects of evil from whatever source, inside or outside ourselves, as he did: open, vulnerable, and loving on the Cross.

26 July   The more one deeply believes what one learns through
Christian teaching, the more one realizes that God can't be boxed
into any one set of human, ego-motivated, structures. He *is* the true
self of every human being he has created, and surely the more we
can reach out to each other externally, the more we'll understand
that.

27 July   [From Melbourne] 'Fragility' and 'experimentation' are
easier in a new country like this. Perhaps they are all the more an
essential witness in our old, somewhat stuck situation in the UK.

28 July I think that if we are to recognize the love of God within us…it is helpful to glimpse something of the way it vastly transcends any concept of love which we can entertain, by seeing it exchanged within the Godhead, and flowing out from it, as depicted in the (Rublev) ikon of the Trinity.

29 July The Gospels are enigmatic, ambiguous, and do not make 'sense'.

30 July In spite of what C. S. Lewis says in *The Great Divorce* I can't really believe that there is personal fulfilment or salvation or true happiness for anyone as long as any soul freely chooses to remain outside the all-embracing, all-suffering love of God. Of course one is almost crushed by the prevailing anti-Godness – whether it takes the form predominantly of violence, greed, aggression, or collusion, it's all a matter of self-getting in opposition to God's self-giving, and just as pernicious in our protected little convent lives as in the high places of arms sales, drug trafficking, and international politics. But at such times it's important…to remember that human solidarity works both ways and that every Godward movement from whatever unlikely source, *is* effective in the divine economy. I am so pleased to be reminded of 'treasure in earthen jars', and that lovely bit of St Paul about seeing no answer to our problems, but not despairing. How *often* it is proved that if one just stays helplessly in a situation, 'things work out', as Father Gilbert says in his last homily.

31 July …before we can be built up in love, we must recognize and repudiate all the unlove that there is in each of us: this means turning from self-pleasing to God-pleasing in practical ways that strip us of self-protectiveness and complacency so that in a measure of humility and penitence we can give ourselves to be used in the contemplative life as God wills.

❖

1 August   I've been thinking quite a lot lately about the fact that I/we thank God when things 'go right', the implication being that when they don't it's due to his displeasure – or incompetence, though one would not want to acknowledge that so baldly! But I suppose really he doesn't see 'right' or 'wrong' (as regards circumstances, not reality) in the way I/we do. Anyway, life happens to us, and I very much doubt that God personally decrees the details of the way it does. I suppose that the scriptural injunction to 'give thanks always for all things' really means being as thoroughly as possible *in* what *is*, and…to affirm God's love in it. And that does not mean trying piously to 'be glad' of horrible things like your accident.

2 August   I sometimes think that we bother too much about what we think, believe, feel, about God. He either is or isn't, quite independently of us, and maybe that's one aspect of his love for the irreplaceable individual each of us is which we don't take enough into account.

3 August   …we should each be ready and open to acknowledge and appreciate every other person as unique and exciting: to draw out the rich potential of their personality, and even to admit that we ourselves can respond beyond our own expectations to the care and interest shown by another. The trouble is that I can acknowledge this in theory, but I am so intrinsically self-centred that usually all I do when I encounter someone else – and certainly the conditions of meeting in community life are usually under some pressure – is to project upon them some aspect of myself…It is so important not to attribute to someone else what would be our own motives for doing whatever she is doing: how hard it is not to judge!

4 August   …evangelism is effective only if what is preached is lived at a cost.

5 August   I'm sure if we try to be faithful and patient God works out his will in his way, which may not seem the best one for us, but probably is.

6 August It is possible to pray for persons and situations with a sense of 'thank goodness it isn't me' until, *in extremis* oneself, it is no longer possible.

7 August Here the provision of hot water as and when possible seems so streamlined that the inconvenience of when it is not possible is minimal – at least for drones on the fringe of things like me! There is something rather surrealistic about the entrails of the dead boiler littered over the garden of Fellowship House: it all increases one's amazed admiration for people who know how these things work.

8 August I find that in everyday life I can see things in proportion more than I used to, and I find a deep peace and joy even in the midst of all the tragedy, suffering, and evil in the world, because I truly believe that the *real* life of every single person is that of the true self of each one of us in the True Vine, and that our ego-motivated outlook and attitudes aren't the ultimate Reality. Of course, the conviction about this gives a basic *good* outlook, but there is the immediate problem caused by the fact that we don't see and understand it, and most people don't seem to want to.

9 August To my mind the impact of the unexpected is the truest form of asceticism. I am aware that I never managed to respond to it adequately and still always do my utmost to stick to *my* plans.

10 August We humans find it terribly hard to acknowledge our contingency. I mean, this is obvious and a truism, but it's part of the ego-centred social system that we have a built-in assumption that we must be capable of and responsible for everything and everyone, and of course we aren't, and can't be.

11 August As regards distractions and wandering thoughts: I find the best thing it to take them with one into prayer, that is, looking towards God with them.

12 August   I can hardly bear to live with myself when I remember things I've done and said, and can't imagine how other people could, or do, bear it now! But then I think, well, one can't know how things were *in toto*, or remember even the whole of one's own part in the picture, let alone allowing for the other people in it to have their own thoughts, words, and actions too. In the end I think it's a question of shoving the mess on to God as usual.

13 August   I well understand that no amount of reassurance from outside, whether given by other people or by circumstances, makes any difference. All depends on how we feel towards ourselves in the depths of ourselves. It's such a blessed relief when one can be at ease about being 'not much good' and 'that sort of person'. I suppose it's our confounded pride that wants our self-esteem to be satisfied. But have you ever met anyone who's *really* self-confident? I generally find that behind the brashest assurances there is fear.

14 August   Whatever we call him, and whether or not we believe in his existence, we have sooner or later to reckon with the devil. As we all know, his aim is to divide, and his chief means of doing so are fear and fogginess, by which I mean a vague unclarity just below the level of consciousness which disquiets us and draws us off course, leading to the dissipation of a deal of spiritual energy in what someone aptly termed 'shadowboxing'. The remedy is first to bring the fears up to the level of consciousness where we can articulate them, at least to ourselves; and then to face them to the extent of taking action where possible. This is so easy to say, and so very hard to do because in our situation it probably means initiating a personal encounter which one is reluctant to do anyway...The very fact of trying is something of a victory for God in us.

15 August   I have appreciated your ruminations about love. Indeed the real thing is in many ways very different from the romantic (and basically selfish!) 'falling in love' experience. And yes, that *is* precious too, the centring of one's whole existence in another person and the whole world turning to gold! I'm sure the reality of a loving relationship with God must be *more than* – it could never be *less than* – that with a human person; and I think the eternal quality of our real engagements with other people is indicated by the fact that when one appreciates the superbness of another in genuine encounter, one always wants more time than the human condition, bounded by limitations, permits. Our 'immortal longings' will be satisfied only in eternity. And surely that – however inconceivable – will have a quality of changing and moving onwards.

16 August   We believe that we are meant to reflect the world at large, and so (of course) we shall fit together as uncomfortably as the rest of humankind on our planet. And we believe that living together in prayer is our primary work, and any pastoral ministry we may have within or outside the Community is peripheral. But we must realize that the fact of our being awkward, opposed, and inharmonious is absolutely right, for we are concerned with conversion of heart and the showing forth of eternal life, not with 'peace at any price'. We must each hold fast to God-centredness in the midst of habitual difficulties, for we cannot expect, or really want, life to be smooth, safe, and secure. But if each of us is really prepared to try to stand alone before God we shall find that there is no such thing as a solitary approach to him. For he has so made us that we can go to Him only in some sort of togetherness. "While the spirit of silence serves to separate each individual life unto God, the spirit of love must ever be binding all together in God, that in the unity of the Spirit all may seek their perfection by holy charity." [*Rule*, chapter 26]

17 August   The 'majesty' of God is that of love triumphing on the Cross and not the pomp we associate with rule and dominion.

18 August   ...the real spirit of silence is a 'loving living' with God, so that we don't need shielding from him by 'escape noise', but are still totally with him in human conversation and life. And this is one hundred per cent by faith, seldom seasoned with 'sight'.

19 August   I find that in my own life it's best not to have too many expectations or to think that one's plans will work out – there should be plenty of room for the eruption of the unexpected. Even in my *very* small-scale existence this applies, and it seems to me that if, perhaps, you could have fewer expectations about what you will accomplish each day, that might ease the tension a bit. I know there are things to be done which are *essential*, full stop. But I wonder if there are others which *you* deem essential but maybe God doesn't? It would be nice to do them if it proves possible, but not disastrous if it doesn't.

20 August   If we are to be built into God's house, we have to be welded into one another by a closeness of relationship that soon shows up as phoney the easy-going tolerance of 'live and let live' which can be mistaken for charity.

21 August   I think you have written out a lot of your anger and been heard; and now that you don't, as you say, have to yell, you can present your insights and perceptions without caring overmuch for other people's reactions. So you can focus most importantly beyond them.

22 August   [In Australia] The sky is fantastic and I could look at it for ever. It calms my frenzied spirit.

23 August   To be concerned with eternal life is not to be 'spiritual' rather than 'earthly'. On the contrary, it is to have a heightened awareness and appreciation of the wonder and glory of creation, and especially of other people. It is to glimpse the reality of living-to-God which alone can goad us into paying the necessary price of 'dying-to-self'. And this results in a radical reorientation of perspective, so that we realize at the back of our minds the knowledge that the assumed values by which we live are not the last word. So the worst that can happen – flood, catastrophe, terrorist massacre, personal disaster – is contained within a love that we can only glimpse by faith but on which we have believed we can stake our lives.

24 August   There is a place, I think, between proclaiming a 'blind faith' that does not dare to question anything and the helpless despair that believes nothing.

25 August   I agree that by the time one gets to the fifties and sixties, one has to accept that one is as one is, and to make the best of it, that is, to think more in terms of finding a way to live with anxiety rather than trying to get rid of it. Perhaps one can go even further, and learn to regard the 'monster' as a 'friend'. For why do we want to rid ourselves of our malaises? Is it not that we might feel more comfortable? But is our business *really* that? Is it not rather to accept the discomfort of not being as we would like to be? It came to me recently that Jesus is with the despairing and the godless, and because we love him, we want to be where he is. So if *we* are in that state, it is in fact 'all right', though by the very nature of the situation it will appear to us as 'all wrong'.

26 August   The concept of death as a means of entering deeper into consciousness, and of Jesus as a man with 'no unconscious', makes a lot of sense. It makes one realize what, in our life's journey, is of lasting value.

27 August   Love has been rightly called 'an outstripping of limits'. It cannot be grasping, possessive, or safe. It must always be ready to go with Jesus into the unexpected and unknown.

28 August   *Ultimately* we know that the blessed bit of God/True Self at the heart of each person (and I hope animals too) can and will and does love and cherish us far better than we, though it won't necessarily result in things being all right in a way we would recognize…If one knows that misery doesn't have the last word, it helps.

29 August   Penitence is something completely other than the guilt or remorse which are self-regarding sicknesses afflicting most of us to some extent, and which must be recognized as such and treated accordingly.

30 August   The discomfort – sometimes it's far more than that – of living 'incomplete' is perhaps the optimum condition for an alive personality: the 'travelling hopefully' image which means inevitably letting go, moving on, change, decay…the sense of moving always onward into what we don't yet know.

31 August   I'm sure this is a rather dark and bewildering time for you. The only thing one can do is to live *in* the present, making a total offering of the situation as it is, which will include the longing that it were otherwise, and accepting it as an opportunity for prayer, and by this deepening of one's givenness and acceptance prepare for whatever God may or may not want later.

1 September   It seems to me that Alan Turing's single-minded pursuit of truth – and that of scientists in general – *is* the purity of heart of the Beatitudes. If he became an atheist, surely it was not so much that scientific truth disproved God (though I suppose it doesn't encourage the understanding of him as personal) as that current religious systems simply don't allow for the hugeness of God who is Love, which encompasses and initiates all that the human mind can discover and invent, and of course a great deal else besides.

2 September   All Christians are committed to fellowship with Christ in the totality of human experience. We must inevitably expect at some point in our lives to know, however dimly, something of the nailedness of the Crucifixion: to be tempted to wriggle out of an intolerable situation, but instead to be held in to it, because that is where Christ is. Personal response to God is the only way of truth at such times. It may well involve refusal to be deflected by our own desires or those of other people around us, and to stay with Christ because we love him, and because staying is the only valid thing to do.

3 September A Dutch scientist is reported to have noted that "to put it simply, the birds are singing much more than Darwin permits," and we in our relative stability of place, have special opportunity to 'stand and stare', and, when we can do this together, to double the delight.

4 September ...how important it is to see one another as individuals, not as a collective. I think one tends instinctively to presume a body of people is in opposition to oneself, whereas directly one meets a person singly one can receive something of his or her uniqueness and appreciate reality in the encounter.

5 September [On loneliness] If it gets embraced, not resisted, it gets transfigured.

6 September I used to tell myself that time *must* pass, and sure enough in five minutes I felt different – not necessarily better! – and that I found helpful.

7 September The solitary life is not something exclusive and elite, for the advanced saint or the way-out eccentric. It is, in fact, one aspect of the Christian way among others, a form of living that proclaims uncompromisingly the basic truth that we all acknowledge in theory – that it is what God does with our lives that matters, and not what we do with them.

8 September Christ's obedience to God did not consist of doing what God told him but of a total oneness with God's disposition of self-giving love.

9 September ...I try somewhat to share the ache, though that will not diminish it. The trouble with God (one of the troubles) is that he will leave us alone in the sort of Gethsemane that Jesus lived through, and resurrection is as remote now as then. And we get our guts torn out and have to go on existing...It'll make sense in time, but not yet: except that 'outside the gate' is God's place.

10 September   [On the blessing of a new building] I feel vaguely disquieted, somehow, about its being deemed appropriate to consecrate everywhere by sprinkling, censing, and 'praying' in ecclesiastical terminology. I feel that God is so much in the nitty gritty of everyday life *everywhere*, not just in supposedly churchy places. It came home to me when I emerged from the bathroom/loo which is to be blessed with some pious utterance about 'sprinkling with clean water': we should say, "Thou shalt *purge* me with hyssop" if anything... 'Religion' gets so sanitized. No wonder the Church is so white and middle class (as we are, mostly, here).

11 September   I live very happily within my limits and travel by wheelchair with expert drivers.

12 September   When I was in Australia, I became convinced, not through reasoning, but by a different kind of 'knowing', that at death the 'I' ceases to be the focus of consciousness. It is something which is quite unimaginable, because now we are so firmly tied into the 'I'. Even when 'I' am looking outside, away from myself, 'I' am aware of 'me' doing it. And I'm not thinking that death means annihilation or absorption, because I'm sure persons go on. I wonder if that makes any sense to you...Father Donald summed it up neatly by saying "there is consciousness, but not self-consciousness." What an *almighty* relief it would be to be shot of the self!

13 September   One of the best things about life is that one never knows what may happen next. So there can always be hope about something turning up; and the unexpected can be fun!

14 September   [Written when in Australia] I had a dream this morning about polishing the Chapter House floor (something which *won't* happen again!) and realized when I woke up (quite happily and matter-of-factly) that here, out of my spiritual 'element', part of me is just not alive. But never mind, there it is...I've *no* doubt of God's closeness and continuing involvement in, and amusement about, what is happening.

15 September   I think we need to have as much (perhaps more) faith in our own 'prayer' as in God. Or rather, we have to trust that, having initiated our self-offering to him, he keeps it going whether or not we're aware of it. So your intention to be pointed Godwards is in itself the 'praying always'. Yes, it is incarnated or articulated, but it is still valid and there even when you are not conscious of repeating your particular phrase of prayer. The whole thing is such a risk...and we can't be sure of anything, I believe. And that makes total commitment to this immense, elusive, unpredictable but utterly magnetic God such fun!

16 September   I quite understand that you have some regrets... That's a basic fact of life, isn't it? There is always a feeling of sadness that some things (or some people) can't 'be', and this is because we have 'immortal longings' and yet are bounded by space and time and mortality. To be all the time with everyone in God: I think that will be the best part of heaven, though perhaps not quite in those worldly terms!

17 September   Someone said to me recently: "I believe your Community has a deeply rooted life of prayer, facing outwards – so that those of us who are outside can be welcomed in." Unless the first part of that statement is true, the rest is worthless. And a deeply rooted life of prayer is going to cost all of us everything we have got, all the time. I think the way into it is for each of us to be willing to be squeezed through the scriptural needle's eye, despoiled of all protection, of all spiritual and other props that are congenial to us, so that we find ourselves nakedly exposed to God in a place that he calls prayer. For us, life in community as nuns and as oblates constitutes the needle: but only God and our own volition can get us through the eye.

18 September   ...maybe humble gratitude is no bad starting point for that universal change of heart which must surely begin with each one of us if it is to bring the fruits of God's redemption of the world.

19 September   I understand what you mean about 'keeping the balance', but honestly, I believe it's best to cut one's losses, recognize that serving God is a 'no win' business, and hand *everything* over to him with a touch of humour. After all, there'd be a risk of complacency if one could ever think one *had* got the balance right.

20 September   ...alas, I see 'naught for your comfort' because you are so right about fear. If one tells oneself it's stupid, it's still got to be lived through. But you *can* name it, even if its name is Mr Terror or Danger Slopes, and face into it, so that it is no longer a 'nameless dread' that 'close behind you treads.' Jolly, isn't it?

21 September   The Holy Spirit will lead us into all truth, and only he knows when and where that journey will be ended. For us there are always fresh depths to be sounded and new paths to be explored, without denying what we have received and the heritage passed on to us. William Temple quotes Bishop Gore as saying that to be inheritors of a great tradition can lead to heroism, but it can also lead to blindness of heart. If we can dare to cultivate a free and fearless exchange among ourselves, our self-deceptions will be shown up and healthily laughed at.

22 September   The true value and purpose of birth, death, and life lie in a realm beyond the reach of our determining. It has been stressed by modern theologians of the Church both in East and West that the Incarnation is "not an answer to sin: it is God's eternal longing to become man, and to make of every human a god out of grace."

23 September   [On hierarchical relationships] ...for each of us there is a delicate balance to be discovered and preserved between being the person we are and duly exercising, with respect for it and for the Community within which it is set, any particular office we may hold for a certain time. (But relationships 'on a par') are notoriously more difficult to develop than 'up and down' ones.

24 September   The knowledge we have of Jesus by faith demands of us conformity to his mind and outlook so that we can be path-finders in the darkness, affirming that the light is there; and that in the midst of temporal life, which has in itself so much that is good and true and beautiful, there is a way into life eternal.

25 September   ...in *any* pastoral role one is dealing with the infinite (that is, persons, made in the divine image) with finite means (that is, limited self and circumstances): so no wonder there is *never* enough time!

26 September   God will be with us whether we wish it or not, and it requires humility on our part to accept his knowledge about areas of ourselves and our activities which we would prefer to keep hidden.

27 September   Words cannot express more than a fraction of what we perceive and experience, and we know that even what we per-ceive is only a fraction of total reality as it is in God. So the truth of the "discipline, prayer, and constant self-oblation" by which we strive "to fill up what is behind of the afflictions of Christ for his Body's sake" is always going to be more than we can articulate, define, or control within an ordered schedule.

28 September   Learning to accept the frustration of our own non-activity helps us to become aware of God's action in us. Above all, if we can still our restless memories and imaginations we shall dis-cover and release the prayer that God himself is making within us, and has been making ceaselessly throughout our lives.

29 September   Taking some intercession time this afternoon, I had a very vivid impression of the *oneness* of the mess, so to speak! We are all concerned with it in our individual experiences, and specific aspects show up according to our circumstances...but basically it's all part of the mire that humankind is working through to come out the other side and find redemption.

30 September   ...it's love-lack that's sinful: not in the sense of 'doing wrong' but of having one's being 'set wrong'.

1 October   (God) will take care of what and who we are becoming, when we stop worrying too much about it.

2 October   When beyond all physical and mental work, even that of living the common life, perhaps all one can do is to be available to God to experience willingly, as a lump of humanity, whatever spiritual situation comes one's way. If one's basic concept of 'good news' is that no one can be further from God than God has been from himself, one can try and accept absences of the sense of God and nevertheless affirm him in them.

3 October   "All of You, nothing of me": the glorious truth of nothing to think about, that is, having to fall for ever through the emptiness and nothingness of *me*, but it *is* in fact the All, the Fulness of the hidden, silent God.

4 October   It is amazing that Jesus doesn't despair of his disciples – or us – in our clottish non-understanding. But his infinite patience takes us as we are where we are, and his time scale is not ours. And he blesses what's done from our feelings and stirrings towards this change of heart which is evident in unexpected forms and people.

5 October   Have three trays: Immediate, Soon, Sometime. And a handy pad of paper on which to scribble things as I think of them to add appropriately. And *try* to turn the light out by 10 p.m. So help me God. Amen.

6 October   ...if we do have to 'point out what is wrong', we must be quite free of our own hurt and irritation before we do so.

7 October [On looking at photographs of Rievaulx and being reminded of a visit there] Soaking in your beautiful photographs gives me the same sort of inarticulable gladness as I recall from my one visit there. I've wallowed in nostalgia and delight: it's been like revisiting beloved places and people.

8 October At times it is tempting to 'get away from it all' and to 'contract out' of twentieth century living...But there is no magic time machine to propel us into some personal and private wonderland. And if there were such a place, we would soon tire of it with no one there but our dissatisfied selves – still victimized by the acute loneliness that prevails in these painful times.

9 October If God doesn't 'intervene' in a way we want and can recognize, we think he's absent. But if only we had eyes to recognize him, we'd find he's utterly there in everything.

10 October For most, the hermitage must be the heart, and our aloneness with God safeguarded deep within the busyness of life. If our disposition is really set towards doing this, difficulties in outward circumstances can turn out to be helps rather than hindrances, because we are starkly faced with the question of whether we are truly 'seeking God first' or simply wanting peace and quiet.

11 October ...however much I may have preached about 'letting go', in the end it has to be *done* to us. It's not just that we don't know what we're holding on to until we lose it; it's that if we *choose* to let go, we're still in control. And it's the loss of *that* that constitutes, I think, the inner, secret renunciations you talk about. So I believe what we have to do is to tell God we are willing for him to 'take...my entire liberty', as St Ignatius put it, and then be ready and willing to live the consequences when he takes us at our word. When I was young and zealous I rather went in for physical penances, as far as was permitted, and I see now *how much* self will, obstinacy, and, probably, arrogance there was in all that.

12 October   Hope does not depend on what one feels, but on how one lives – and *wills* to live; and God's love is inexorably enduring.

13 October   On meeting the 'black dog' of depression: I find myself that the best treatment is to walk up to the beast and even pat it, as no one can ever banish it satisfactorily.

14 October   Praying…means not simply washing our hands of the problems (we face) and passing (them) on to God as 'too difficult', but living with the consequences of confusion and contradiction, those within ourselves as well as amongst ourselves, and continuing to affirm God in the midst of it all.

15 October   In the course of our Christian discipleship, most of us find that when we try, however rumblingly, to follow God's way, he takes us at our word and one bottom or another falls out of our lives. We are left with a love which depends not on his doing for us what we had hoped and expected, but on the glimpse we have had of a Person who originally claimed our allegiance and retains it because of what we believe about him.

16 October   It's so hard, when in the midst of other people's expectations (not to mention *demands*), to remember and *live by* the fact that we can best serve them by giving ourselves wholeheartedly to God and affirming our readiness to be used by him in a work that only he can do, and we can't. Left to ourselves, it's obvious and easy to accept, but in the whirl of twentieth century Western life it's *not*.

17 October   Companionship: When helpless to change situations or convince people from outside about something they cannot believe inside, we can freely *be there* for them. We can give this to God and creatures. Perhaps it is a genuine expression of Love. "*Ich will hier bei Dir stehen.*" Stay with it and don't try to escape, shirk, or alter-to-improve one's feelings if a blackness descends: accepting it and attempting to endure it can possibly be used by God as intercession. Parents who have to see their children hurting themselves and can't interfere can be there for them; those unjustly accused and mis-understood, when all reasonable attempts at communication fail can at least say *"bei die...Ich will hier bei Dir stehen."* Emmanuel – God with us. It's what God says to us and lives and dies for us – that's what love is.

18 October "Discipleship is not limited to what you can compre-hend – it must transcend all comprehension. Plunge into the deep waters...Bewilderment is the true comprehension. Not to know where you are going is the true knowledge..." Martin Luther's words apply truly to our living together...he saw that what he wished to articulate must, in the end, remain a mystery. If we understood what happens in our life we should not be living it prop-erly. We do know that there are spiritual thorns and boulders, that we get pricked or stub our toes if we try to build a nest for ourselves, that there are too many people and there is not enough room. But we know too that if we are ready to allow space for one another, the desert can blossom like a rose, and if our wilderness is a place where the evil in each of us can be absorbed and contained, not sparking off an endless chain of reactions, then we can be used by God in the redemption of the world.

19 October Our chief way of protest is not to do something drastic, but to try deliberately to live in opposition to the pressures of comfort, compromise, and 'cleverness' (in the sense of 'double-mindedness') which dominate the world. "Purity of heart is to will one thing," and that, says Kierkegaard, means unswerving, single-minded pursuit of the Good.

20 October About this 'evil' business. Again, I think one's got to leave it to God, in faith. If we have quite seriously told him we're willing to be used in his purposes of reconciliation, and to take the consequences, he will respect that. I doubt it we will ever 'know' what is happening in the way we would like. I don't think we can say, "Now I am engaged in spiritual conflict. Spot on." (I don't mean to be overly frivolous, but I think you'll know what I'm getting at.) It's more likely to be a sense of weight and oppression, which may or may not be immediately explicable by some personal circumstances. Or it may be acute awareness of one's own nastiness, part of the large lump of humanness, in which one has to say 'God', however reluctantly. You may perhaps be psychically sensitive to specific evidences of evil: in which case, be canny. Father Gilbert always warned us not to be *curious*, trying to specify what was happening and why, also not to be frightened. One can claim the armour of God by reciting some portion of psalmody or other scripture, or St Patrick's Breastplate. I think it's best not to seek out this sort of thing because there *is* the danger of fantasy and one's 'private world', as you say. Leave it to God, and don't mind what you do or do not know about what he is doing with you.

21 October   You say that God has a lot to answer for. I don't know why I felt I must spring to his defence, as though he either needed it or wanted it. But I think it is part of God's 'kenosis', self-emptying, to have such a bad press image…God is himself broken and given, and so he totally accepts and enters into that view and pays the price and experiences the consequences. I do think God lives and dies it all, whether or not we can shake our fist at him. And there are plenty of 'out of knowledge' witnesses to his being with the dumb and inarticulate sufferers, inside their skin, so to speak, not magically to alleviate the agony…I suppose we just have to take it on trust, because God himself hasn't shirked the consequences, that it is all in aid of (perhaps an expression of) a love that is unrecognizable as such to us because we haven't begun to see the reality and the plus side of self-sacrifice as lived by God.

22 October   A background of Godwardness *isn't* expendable, though 'plonk' times can certainly vary in duration – even five minutes is worthwhile and a daily 'must' to make the statement about God mattering most…Keep looking steadily Godwards even if he/she is in a dark cloud. You don't necessarily have to be heroic, in fact quite the reverse, clownish and defeated.

23 October 'Perfection' is not good behaviour but God-centredness.

24 October I agree that one's past has to be owned, together with its consequences, but almost inevitably, I find, one's memory distorts events, so that too much thinking is not good, and one has to find how to convince the memories that one is not ignoring them, but also not over-encouraging them.

25 October The virtue of giving is so much emphasized...that we easily forget the primary importance of being able to receive...(I)n order to give to God and to one another the 'one thing necessary' – ourselves – we have to be ready to let go of a great deal of protective clutter at many levels. That is the only way we can be empty enough to receive the love and truth of God.

26 October [When ill during a visit to Australia] In (the Chaplain's) absence on holiday I've made it quite clear that I'm very happy to have a sister come rather than a priest, and when the sacristan does, we have the little service appointed in the Australian Prayer Book and I can do one of the readings. And I suddenly found what corporate participation really means. Of course the actual reading wasn't essential, but the *celebration among peers*. I wasn't an object, desperately unworthy as the grovel prayers of the 1928 Prayer Book left beyond doubt, being done good to.

27 October It is so hard to 'confess' by formula, sacramentally or otherwise, because what one wants to acknowledge is an awareness of an existential alienation which is beyond articulation. Psalm 51 is perhaps the nearest we can get to this. For when I list my misdeeds I can to some extent still be in control.

28 October Just as we all know that those following the solitary life are making explicit something basically inherent to the vocation of each one of us, so I would contend that every hermit is irrevocably bound up in and forms part of the common life of the Sisters of the Love of God. For we must never forget that we have been called into community, and of our own free wills have said Yes to that call, probably just because most of us would have vastly preferred to plough our own furrows, 'seeking God only' on our terms, rubbing shoulders amiably enough, maybe, with our neighbours, but ultimately keeping ourselves to our individual selves.

29 October   Remember that God is good at 'writing straight with crooked lines', and that is all that most of us give him the chance to do!

30 October   But do not let us forget that there is, intended for all, a lower, 'sub-clutter', level of prayer which is the true response of every person to the Creator. Experience of this does not depend on temperament or circumstances, and if it comes it is wholly gift. It turns the world and ourselves upside down because it puts us in a place where what normally 'matters' does so no longer. For an instant outside of time we know all things to be made by and for God and held for ever in him. We have not come here to 'enjoy' this sort of prayer, perhaps not necessarily to experience it: but belief in the reality of the dimension it affirms forms the basis of the contemplative life and builds up each one of us in dependence on God expressed by 'praying always', however he gradually leads us into doing this.

31 October   While each of us can rightly apply all that Psalm 51 says to ourselves personally, it can and should be used as an expression of solidarity with the whole sinful world. For this to be more than a pious thought we must claim and know our own particular involvement, accepting that we cannot escape complicity in responsibility for the whole world's being as it is.

1 November ...prayer is not a last ditch hope when all else fails. Prayer is, rather, a universal force for mustering the Light of Christ to quell the powers of darkness around the world.

2 November Perhaps it is not altogether unreasonable to think that when we come to physical death we shall find some element of familiarity, whether or not we have known God in terms of 'religion'. Apprehensions of truth and beauty in any form touch what we feel to be imperishable. It is hard to believe that in their deepest and dearest aspects human relationships do not endure beyond death.

3 November I think that God's 'loving care' of us does *not* mean keeping us comfortable or even aware of him. Pain and death are so much part of the universe, aren't they? All very well to *say* this in my snug comfort...

4 November We see, according to St Paul, only 'in a glass, darkly'. When we are able to accept that, it can be quite a relief to stop trying vainly to grasp things in the round and so to exercise control over them. How often it happens that our actual experience of people or events is very different from what we have anticipated. We can be agonizingly apprehensive or foolishly sanguine beforehand, and then be surprised, pleasantly or unpleasantly.

But there is more than this where other people are concerned: however we think of them in absence, their presence introduces an element we cannot bargain for. We find that, for instance, the fear or anger we have been harbouring – or our innate and reprehensible suspicion of strangers – melts away if something of a smile comes into the situation.

5 November Human love is seldom merely a neatly reciprocal matter of mutual exchange. It is a mystery which is diminished by attempts at definition. But when we receive (love) from one person, we are, more often than not, enabled to give in our turn to another.

6 November   I'm sure you *do* in fact 'have the answer' in so far as
you see that it consists in not having it – and not even wanting it,
because in fact there is no such thing as 'the answer'. I can imagine
that if *only* your fellow clergy could reach that same conclusion,
they'd be happier! Oh dear – our Protestant Northern European
tradition is such a tiresome heritage. We must preserve a 'front'.

7 November   The heart of the life of prayer is *stillness*, and that
comes from a genuine acceptance of the present moment *as it is*,
even though it might go right against the grain. If you can build on
this, you will find tranquillity and room for growth in prayer even
in the hubbub, whereas it's possible to wreck the stillness of out-
wardly 'ideal' conditions by inner anxieties and revolts.

8 November   We tend to be very sure we know what another person
ought to be, and how she should become thus. The recognition and
building up of one another into what God intends each to be, discovering and developing her potential by our belief and delight in
her, is a very real part of our own growth, and, as we so often preach
but do not always practise, it involves giving space to others rather
than taking it for ourselves. It means, too, accepting the untidy,
unsatisfactory situation of belonging to a group of real people.

9 November   I think one's own finitude, transience, and unknowing
are a consequence of God's all-ness, don't you? It's hard to accept;
and saying 'yes' with one's whole being and one's life is no easy
matter because that very life is unpredictable, and we don't know
what God in his all-ness is going to allow or require next. Somehow
or other the conviction that he is Love, and all his purposes are that,
is central, and must be grasped by the will, if it can't by reason.

10 November   Fear is the biggest bugbear for most of us, I think.
You are able to analyse your situation pretty clearly, which indicates
that you are on top ot it, not it of you. And I am a great believer in
naming adversaries. I even make lists of current concerns and
coming dreads. But then I have to balance all that with a list of

uncovenanted mercies which have come out of the blue and taken me by surprise...An unfazed 'frightful fiend' (to use a phrase of Coleridge) is most debilitating spiritually and psychologically. But you do know where you are, and yes, the casting out *would* be freeing and a relief. But what is *your* blessed 'thorn in the flesh' which makes you aware of the sufficiency of God's grace and that his strength is indeed made perfect in our weakness?

11 November ...there can be a sort of creative surrender to the present moment which somehow sanctifies it, and is not just bowing to the inevitable, so that accepting non-ideal situations is not necessarily a 'second best' but utterly the right way forward. I find that in the end what I could have considered a better situation would not have been.

12 November I know what you mean about 'living what one speaks', but it's important not to wait to speak until one thinks one is doing that.

13 November Create an environment that is numinous rather than clinical.

14 November ...Christ and his followers have *no* enemies. We are all in one another, and as God's love embraces all, so must we. We can hold different opinions and dislike one another's views and actions. But always there must be deep love and acceptance of every *person*. And the work of the contemplative is to hold the consequences of that in personal experience.

15 November It seems a real work of reconciliation to embrace not only death but even the evil, universally feared and loathed cancer which is inexorably consuming her. Perhaps by the same token that's what you have to do with the nastiness that assails you You write wisely that at one point you let it sweep over you and glimpsed grace in the midst of it. I think that a lot of reconciliation is about accepting, not disposing of, the pain of being beastly.

16 November   It's really costly to 'be there' for someone else, to give time and attention, often when it *interrupts* something else one's doing or has planned. I still can't do that!

17 November   We must believe in one another's good intentions, even when we do seem to be unloving, and not make too much fuss about the inevitable hurts we all sustain. Whatever happens God can use; whatever wrongness we create can be given to him for transfiguration; for with it we give the rest of the lump of hurt and wrongness in the world.

18 November   Our prayer may be dark, dry, and dismal, but that does not matter as long as we are learning to be more and more exposed to difficulties – in life as well as in prayer – through such experiences of the desert. Growth in accepting discomfort may seem a modest sort of achievement, but at least it is movement.

19 November   How true it is that "for us there is only the trying – the rest is not our business." If we are trying to hand over the control of ourselves to God in order to be used by him in his infinitely vast purposes of reconciliation, we can know that although our trust in him will be tested to the uttermost, it will never be betrayed. He meets us at the point of our deepest desire – often beyond our own articulation – brings us to a pitch of sensitivity where we are conscious of the fears, uncertainties, and anxieties which have to be kept just below the surface in most people's ways of life, and asks us to affirm his love through it all.

20 November   The effect of words on their hearers and readers is not always directly related to the meaning they contain, and the deliberate or inadvertent misinterpretation of what is spoken and written by other people is one of the hazards of these hazardous times. The power of language consists in more than the factual accuracy – or otherwise – of what it conveys, because it affects the emotions as well as the intelligence, and communication operates at many levels, conscious and unconscious.

We can diminish a concept or an experience by trying to articulate what words cannot capture. Words can also be used in such a way as to evoke something beyond what is actually said. Obviously, literary skills can be misused and orators can wax eloquent in praise or blame of the same set of facts, so that the victims of verbal bombardment are left wondering what is the precise relationship of word and meaning...Alice had the same problem when communicating with Humpty Dumpy!

21 November   I wonder if, perhaps, in your lowest times, when, I imagine, one of the worst aspects is a sense of isolation, you can bring yourself deliberately to claim kinship with all the *many* people of goodwill that are everywhere on the side of light. I am sure it must be a good thing to do consciously at dire moments.

22 November   If we dress ourselves up in ready-made clothing that does not fit us and was never meant to fit us, we should not be surprised if we're permanently uncomfortable.

23 November   ...to suffer the unfolding of events...is sometimes well nigh intolerable, and one almost jumps off the cross to *do* something about it.

24 November   I expect there are times when many of the baptized who take Christianity seriously wish that they need not do so. For believing that God is truly involved with humankind in the way shown by Jesus means that we are offered the opportunity to be truly involved in God's redemptive work. So we have the option of deciding whether or not to respond by accepting the consequences, and knowing also 'the fellowship of his sufferings'.

25 November   Inevitably, the tenor of all religious exhortation is that if you will do what is recommended, not only good behaviour but loving God, you will 'feel good'. But you don't. Nevertheless, God asserts himself, humorously, through the conviction that it's OK if you don't.

26 November   It's good to remember God's around. He'll have to cope. I can't!

27 November   Father Gilbert Shaw reminded the Community that our work is listening – taking the situation we are in and "holding it in courage, not being beaten down by it." Our work is "standing," he said, "holding things without being deflected by your own desires or the desires of other people. Then things work out."

It would be well for all Christians to learn to listen in that way for the sort of deepening in prayer that could bring about in us a change of heart and even of mind. The penitential seasons throughout the church year give us ready-made opportunities to practise self-denial and the discipline of more acute listening to God and to people. But we can approach true 'conversion of heart' in yet another way, redirecting our entire life to the will of God rather than by imposing conditions on ourselves, as we are inclined to do, just for a day or a season...

28 November   When we consent to go out from what is safe and familiar to meet what is new and mysterious, we remove something of what blocks the way between our hearts and God.

29 November   [During a lonely and difficult time for the recipient] ...just a huge hug and lots of love and tender loving care – and none of it's any damn use at all, is it? So wot.

30 November   There is so much more in 'meeting' than the spoken words exchanged...We set so much store by verbalization – written and spoken – and perhaps what is more important cannot be expressed that way.

❖

1 December   Be still in the hurt, and stay with it, and let God gestate and grow in you, and let the end product of creativity be his first, and yours enablingly.

2 December   If Christians are to grasp anew something of God's good news, it will be in the context of belonging to the human lump. If we learn something more about experiencing here and now the dimensions of life eternal...it will be through relationships with other people as well as with God.

People are real at a level deeper and more durable than anything we are able to perceive.

3 December   Of course the love and friendship − why can't I say 'my' when I mean it?! − abide, whenever, whatever, how much you write. Also what passes (it has to!) for 'prayer'. For all of you.

4 December   ...one aspect of togetherness with God is growing into companionable variety with other people, learning not to fear opinions other than one's own.

5 December   "They also serve who only stand and wait." Perhaps the condition of desolation can be used if we accept what is happening, body, mind, and spirit, and claim Christ's redemption of it all. And keep on keeping on.

6 December   World poverty should certainly drive us to examine ourselves on our practice of spiritual poverty which probably leaves much to be desired when we really look at it. How many ideas, ideals, principles am I clinging to? Why should I have the satisfaction and security of feeling that I am in the right place? Why should I not know spiritual impoverishment through doubts and desolations in the way that others suffer material destitution? But this does not exempt us from feeling uncomfortable that we are part of an affluent society, and this salutary discomfort can be made an occasion for deepening our prayer, sharing this and other situations at a point where it hurts, and holding all to God in a stillness that does not seek to alleviate the pain by thinking of self-soothing remedies or excuses. And there is the other side: we need not be afraid of beauty and the good things of God's and man's creation. Provided we are really set to love God above all things, we can quite safely love him in them too.

7 December   There is no experience of joy or sorrow, no anguish about another's grief and our own helplessness to help, no sense of utter estrangement from God himself in which God has not reached that place before us, so as to be in it with us. That is why 'conversion of heart' means, for everyone, simply being willing to acknowledge before God – to the full extent that we can see – who and what we are, and our readiness to offer him the sum total. Only so can we bring to him for healing the passions of human nature that divide families, societies, and nations, and that seem likely to destroy the world.

8 December   We start, with the rest of humankind and with our incarnate Lord himself, from a place of fear, because that is where the world is. But if we consent, for and in and with his love, to go headlong into the worst that can happen (or, less dramatically and more realistically, to accept that in our community life we cannot have everything to our liking) we shall find that not only do we have nothing to lose and against which to protect ourselves, but that our perspectives have changed.

9 December   I think I can dimly glimpse what Jesus means about loving one another as he loves us, that is, from the true self. That's terribly demanding, isn't it? Actually, I find it rather a relief that the facile benevolence which I can quite easily distribute and call 'love' is *not* what is required.

10 December   When, in community life, events and people recur constantly, you're bound to experience ups and downs – and to survive the latter. It's really only the ego that suffers them, and, actually, I find it rather a relief to 'fall short'.

11 December   There is more validity in travelling hopefully than in arriving, in disposition than in acts, in existence of relationship than in encounters, in intuitive apprehension of God's dimension than in God talk.

12 December   During Advent we wait and watch and hope for what has already happened, appeared, and been realized in the historical birth of Jesus Christ. But if we can enlarge our awareness we can become alert to what is continually new and surprising. By contrast, because I am habitually anxious I tend to arrive early for trains and appointments, and my 'waiting' is fraught with frustration and impatience.

If I were more able to live light-heartedly and peacefully in the present moment – which, I maintain, includes awareness of the one before and the one after – perhaps there would be more of preparation in the truest, deepest sense: not just trying to get things done before Christmas, but quietly watching as one does for the dawn, noticing the streaks of light appearing in the sky and the first squawks of early birds.

13 December   We have to be perpetually aware that in our way of life, which gives much opportunity for thought, the devil will insinuate evil suggestions which fester and proliferate until we become a prey, before we know it, to all kinds of fantastic imaginings which we cannot conceive to be anything but the sober truth. The sovereign here is to keep a sense of proportion, which means a sense of humour that can make us laugh at ourselves; and also, directly we find ourselves thinking negatively, and that something 'isn't fair', to turn to God and try to put in some positive thought about him instead.

14 December   When tempted to despair of the human condition I take comfort from the fact that it's still *bad* things that make the news, and I think of all the good and lovely things about human nature that crop up unexpectedly.

15 December   The loss of control over *body*...comes as a salutary shock...The loss of control over *mind* will be even harder because I won't be able to analyse it, and while I'm still responsible I must say Yes to the prospect of being underneath that and *failing* in the Yes...(With mild temporary losses with migraine, it's no good fussing.)

16 December   The chiselling of the bricks for building involves discovering and blocking up our own particular escape routes, praying for stability and perseverance, and facing and accepting reality.

17 December   It's odd, isn't it, how essential to the Body are those who appear to be thorns in the flesh.

18 December   The end of life *is* tough, isn't it? I suppose we aren't able to cope with its demands until we get there! No short cuts.

19 December   [I was struck recently] by Jesus saying to Pilate, "My kingdom is not of this world," and thinking how many million times each second people pray, "Thy kingdom come." Do we really *want* the radical reversal of all our assumed values that that 'world' would entail?

20 December   Shoot off an arrow whenever you feel like it. We're a sitting target!

21 December   I truly think that the highest form of ministry is to listen, don't you? It may not seem all that great to the do-er, but it's one hundred per cent better for the 'done-to' than what the do-er might wish to inflict.

22 December   It's awkward when you can see both sides of all questions, isn't it? One just *has* to make up one's mind to cut one's losses somewhere as it isn't possible in our finite state to eat and have cake.

23 December At Christmas time we think especially of the Incarnation in respect of the ineffable God being of us and with us. Perhaps we should follow this thought to an enduring organization of the infinite potential and impenetrable mystery of every one of our fellow human beings.

24 December When it comes to Christmas we are all children again: at least, in so far as we allow ourselves to succumb to the spontaneous delight of receiving something as sheer gift and just enjoying it.

25 December God shows his love for us by taking a vast risk, and each Christmas we are jolted into looking at it afresh. He 'empties himself' and puts himself into our hands, so that we can reject and refuse him, misunderstand and abuse him, manipulate and use him. Or we can try, by his grace, to respond with a love that does, however feebly, take its character from his.

26 December I believe a Christian's business is to be ready to be entered, by God, into the human condition on *his* terms, as *he* wishes, and so to extend the Incarnation.

27 December Decision making is always difficult: there's often no clear 'right way' and there will always be regrets whichever way one decides. I think generally God doesn't mind much *what* we choose and is more concerned with the *why*.

28 December We do tend…to give material aid and information and advice rather than the one thing necessary: companionship. That's the most costly thing to give…because it requires time and attention which (this) one used usually to have other plans for! But I believe any genuine love must have in it an element of the self-less, don't you? Again I have to speak from personal experience when I say how easily one scatters 'love' around which won't bear much testing! And I *do* agree, we need to attend more to receiving.

29 December   I don't think God has 'a will' for us that we can know clearly and be safe! A sister quoted to me Alan Harrison's saying: "I think God says, 'You choose, and I'll be with you,' " which seems wise to me. So I suppose one has to do the best one can according to one's lights and inclination, knowing one's motives are probably mixed, and ready to backtrack if that seems the wrong way.

30 December   [On her love of pigs] Their benevolent sleepiness appeals to me.

31 December   I have a lovely ground floor room looking straight out on to the garden. So I watch the nearby fruit trees, skeletal at present, developing first bumps, then blossom, then leaves, then fruit. I'm so constantly and overwhelmingly grateful for this bonus – an uncovenanted mercy – of having time to lie back and stare!

SOURCES

JANUARY

1 Fourteenth Chapter Charge, 1986
2 A private letter, reproduced with permission
3 Second Chapter Charge, 1974
4 Read by Mother Anne at the Memorial Eucharist for Sr Jane on 27 May 1995
5 Fairacres Chronicle
6 Fairacres Chronicle
7 Sixth Chapter Charge, 1978
8 Twelfth Chapter Charge, 1984
9 Twelfth Chapter Charge, 1984
10 A private letter, reproduced with permission
11 A private letter, reproduced with permission
12 A talk on the Spirit of Love, 1978
13 Fairacres Chronicle
14 A private letter, reproduced with permission
15 Eighth Chapter Charge, 1980
16 A private letter, reproduced with permission
17 A private letter, reproduced with permission
18 A private letter, reproduced with permission
19 Thirteenth Chapter Charge, 1985
20 A private letter, reproduced with permission
21 Tenth Chapter Charge, 1982
22 Fairacres Chronicle
23 A private letter, reproduced with permission
24 A private letter, reproduced with permission
25 A letter to her sisters, 1982
26 Some personal annotations on the Community's Rule, 1989
27 A private letter, reproduced with permission
28 A private letter, reproduced with permission
29 Ninth Chapter Charge, 1981
30 Some personal annotations on the Community's Rule, 1989
31 A private letter, reproduced with permission

FEBRUARY

1   Fairacres Chronicle
2   Some personal annotations on the Community's Rule, 1989
3   Some personal annotations on the Community's Rule, 1989
4   Tenth Chapter Charge, 1982
5   Some personal annotations on the Community's Rule, 1989
6   Fourth Chapter Charge, 1976
7   A private letter, reproduced with permission
8   Fairacres Chronicle
9   Tenth Chapter Charge, 1982
10   Fairacres Chronicle
11   Fourteenth Chapter Charge, 1986
12   Sixth Chapter Charge, 1978
13   Second Chapter Charge, 1972
14   Fifth Chapter Charge, 1977
15   Some personal annotations on the Community's Rule, 1989
16   Read by Mother Anne at the Memorial Eucharist for Sr Jane
       on 27 May 1995
17   Fairacres Chronicle
18   A private letter, reproduced with permission
19   Fourth Chapter Charge, 1976
20   Fifth Chapter Charge, 1977
21   A talk on the Spirit of Love, 1978
22   Fairacres Chronicle
23   A letter to the Community, 1979
24   Fairacres Chronicle
25   Fourth Chapter Charge, 1976
26   A private letter, reproduced with permission
27   A private letter, reproduced with permission
28   Marginalia
29   A letter to her sisters, 1976

MARCH

1   Fairacres Chronicle
2   Quoted by Bishop Robert Runcie at the Memorial Eucharist for
       Sr Jane on 27 May 1995
3   A private letter, reproduced with permission
4   A private letter, reproduced with permission

11 Fairacres Chronicle
12 Fifth Chapter Charge, 1977
13 Ninth Chapter Charge, 1981
14 Some personal annotations on the Community's Rule, 1989
15 A letter to her sisters, 1979
16 A private letter, reproduced with permission
17 Third Chapter Charge, 1975
18 Some personal annotations on the Community's Rule, 1989
19 Second Chapter Charge, 1974
20 Some personal annotations on the Community's Rule, 1989
21 A private letter, reproduced with permission
22 Ninth Chapter Charge, 1981
23 A private letter, reproduced with permission
24 First Chapter Charge, 1973
25 A private letter, reproduced with permission
26 Some personal annotations on the Community's Rule, 1989
27 Twelfth Chapter Charge, 1984
28 A private letter, reproduced with permission
29 Eleventh Chapter Charge, 1983
30 A private letter, reproduced with permission

MAY

1   Seventh Chapter Charge, 1979
2   A private letter, reproduced with permission
3   A private letter, reproduced with permission
4   Tenth Chapter Charge, 1982
5   A private letter, reproduced with permission
6   Fifteenth Chapter Charge, 1987
7   A private letter, reproduced with permission
8   A private letter, reproduced with permission
9   A private letter, reproduced with permission
10 Fourth Chapter Charge, 1976
11 A private letter, reproduced with permission
12 A private letter, reproduced with permission
13 A private letter, reproduced with permission
14 Fairacres Chronicle
15 A private letter, reproduced with permission
16 A private letter, reproduced with permission
17 A private letter, reproduced with permission

18 Read by Mother Anne at the Memorial Eucharist for Sr Jane on 27 May 1995
19 Fairacres Chronicle
20 Third Chapter Charge, 1975
21 Fourth Chapter Charge, 1976
22 Some personal annotations on the Community's Rule, 1989
23 Eighth Chapter Charge, 1980
24 A private letter, reproduced with permission
25 Twelfth Chapter Charge, 1984
26 Fourth Chapter Charge, 1976
27 A private letter, reproduced with permission
28 A private letter, reproduced with permission
29 Eighth Chapter Charge, 1980
30 A private letter, reproduced with permission
31 A private letter, reproduced with permission

JUNE

1 A private letter, reproduced with permission
2 A private letter, reproduced with permission
3 Fifth Chapter Charge, 1977
4 Fifth Chapter Charge, 1977
5 A private letter, reproduced with permission
6 Fairaces Chronicle
7 A private letter, reproduced with permission
8 A talk on the Spirit of Love, 1978
9 Fairaces Chronicle
10 Ninth Chapter Charge, 1981
11 Fairaces Chronicle
12 Some personal annotations on the Community's Rule, 1989
13 Some personal annotations on the Community's Rule, 1989
14 Fairaces Chronicle
15 Some personal annotations on the Community's Rule, 1989
16 A private letter, reproduced with permission
17 Fairaces Chronicle
18 A private letter, reproduced with permission
19 A private letter, reproduced with permission
20 A private letter, reproduced with permission
21 Fifth Chapter Charge, 1977
22 Fairaces Chronicle

23 First Chapter Charge, 1973
24 A private letter, reproduced with permission
25 Fairaces Chronicle
26 Fairaces Chronicle
27 Sixth Chapter Charge, 1978
28 Thirteenth Chapter Charge, 1985
29 A private letter, reproduced with permission
30 Fifteenth Chapter Charge, 1987

JULY

1 Second Chapter Charge, 1974
2 A private letter, reproduced with permission
3 A private letter, reproduced with permission
4 A private letter, reproduced with permission
5 A private letter, reproduced with permission
6 Fairacres Chronicle
7 Twelfth Chapter Charge, 1984
8 A private letter, reproduced with permission
9 Third Chapter Charge, 1975
10 First Chapter Charge, 1973
11 Fairacres Chronicle
12 Thirteenth Chapter Charge, 1985
13 Fairacres Chronicle
14 Fairacres Chronicle
15 Some personal annotations on the Community's Rule, 1989
16 A private letter, reproduced with permission
17 A talk on the Spirit of Love, 1978
18 Twelfth Chapter Charge, 1984
19 Eighth Chapter Charge, 1980
20 Fairacres Chronicle
21 A private letter, reproduced with permission
22 First Chapter Charge, 1973
23 A private letter, reproduced with permission
24 Fairacres Chronicle
25 Fairacres Chronicle
26 A private letter, reproduced with permission
27 A private letter, reproduced with permission
28 Fifth Chapter Charge, 1977

29 Some personal annotations on the Community's Rule, 1989
30 A private letter, reproduced with permission
31 First Chapter Charge, 1973

AUGUST

 1 A private letter, reproduced with permission
 2 A private letter, reproduced with permission
 3 A talk on the Spirit of Love, 1978
 4 Some personal annotations on the Community's Rule, 1989
 5 A private letter, reproduced with permission
 6 Some personal annotations on the Community's Rule, 1989
 7 From a letter to her sisters, 1982
 8 A private letter, reproduced with permission
 9 A private letter, reproduced with permission
10 A private letter, reproduced with permission
11 A private letter, reproduced with permission
12 A private letter, reproduced with permission
13 A private letter, reproduced with permission
14 Sixth Chapter Charge, 1978
15 A private letter, reproduced with permission
16 A talk on the Spirit of Love, 1978
17 Some personal annotations on the Community's Rule, 1989
18 Some personal annotations on the Community's Rule, 1989
19 A private letter, reproduced with permission
20 First Chapter Charge, 1973
21 A private letter, reproduced with permission
22 A private letter, reproduced with permission
23 A talk on the Spirit of Love, 1978
24 A private letter, reproduced with permission
25 A private letter, reproduced with permission
26 A private letter, reproduced with permission
27 Fairacres Chronicle
28 Fairacres Chronicle
29 Fairacres Chronicle
30 A private letter, reproduced with permission
31 A private letter, reproduced with permission

SEPTEMBER

1   A private letter, reproduced with permission
2   Fairacres Chronicle
3   Third Chapter Charge, 1975
4   A talk on the Spirit of Love, 1978
5   A private letter, reproduced with permission
6   A private letter, reproduced with permission
7   Fairacres Chronicle
8   Some personal annotations on the Community's Rule, 1989
9   A private letter, reproduced with permission
10 A private letter, reproduced with permission
11 A private letter, reproduced with permission
12 A private letter, reproduced with permission
13 A private letter, reproduced with permission
14 A private letter, reproduced with permission
15 A private letter, reproduced with permission
16 A private letter, reproduced with permission
17 Tenth Chapter Charge, 1982
18 A private letter, reproduced with permission
19 A private letter, reproduced with permission
20 A private letter, reproduced with permission
21 Ninth Chapter Charge, 1981
22 Fairacres Chronicle
23 A talk on the Spirit of Love, 1978
24 Fairacres Chronicle
25 A private letter, reproduced with permission
26 Fairacres Chronicle
27 Fifteenth Chapter Charge, 1987
28 Fairacres Chronicle
29 A private letter, reproduced with permission
30 A private letter, reproduced with permission

OCTOBER

1   Sixth Chapter Charge, 1978
2   Some personal annotations on the Community's Rule, 1989
3   Some personal annotations on the Community's Rule, 1989
4   Some personal annotations on the Community's Rule, 1989
5   Some personal annotations on the Community's Rule, 1989

6   A retreat address
7   A private letter, reproduced with permission
8   Fairaces Chronicle
9   Some personal annotations on the Community's Rule, 1989
10 Fourteenth Chapter Charge, 1986
11 A private letter, reproduced with permission
12 A private letter, reproduced with permission
13 A private letter, reproduced with permission
14 Fairaces Chronicle
15 Fairaces Chronicle
16 A private letter, reproduced with permission
17 Marginalia
18 Fourth Chapter Charge, 1976
19 Third Chapter Charge, 1975
20 A private letter, reproduced with permission
21 A private letter, reproduced with permission
22 A private letter, reproduced with permission
23 Some personal annotations on the Community's Rule, 1989
24 A private letter, reproduced with permission
25 Fairaces Chronicle
26 A private letter, reproduced with permission
27 Some personal annotations on the Community's Rule, 1989
28 Fifth Chapter Charge, 1977
29 A private letter, reproduced with permission
30 Twelfth Chapter Charge, 1984
31 Fairaces Chronicle

NOVEMBER

1   Fairaces Chronicle
2   A private letter, reproduced with permission
3   A private letter, reproduced with permission
4   Fairaces Chronicle
5   Fairaces Chronicle
6   A private letter, reproduced with permission
7   A private letter, reproduced with permission
8   A private letter, reproduced with permission
9   A private letter, reproduced with permission
10 A private letter, reproduced with permission
11 A private letter, reproduced with permission

12   A private letter, reproduced with permission
13   A private letter, reproduced with permission
14   Some personal annotations on the Community's Rule, 1989
15   A private letter, reproduced with permission
16   Marginalia
17   Fifteenth Chapter Charge, 1987
18   First Chapter Charge, 1973
19   Thirteenth Chapter Charge, 1985
20   Fairaces Chronicle
21   A private letter, reproduced with permission
22   Quoted by Bishop Robert Runcie at the Memorial Eucharist for
      Sr Jane on 27 May 1995
23   A private letter, reproduced with permission
24   Fairaces Chronicle
25   Some personal annotations on the Community's Rule, 1989
26   A private letter, reproduced with permission
27   Fairaces Chronicle
28   Fairaces Chronicle
29   A private letter, reproduced with permission
30   A private letter, reproduced with permission

DECEMBER

1   A private letter, reproduced with permission
2   Fairacres Chronicle
3   A private letter, reproduced with permission
4   Read by Mother Anne at the Memorial Eucharist for Sr Jane
      on 27 May 1995
5   Some personal annotations on the Community's Rule, 1989
6   First Chapter Charge, 1973
7   Fairacres Chronicle
8   Eighth Chapter Charge, 1980
9   A private letter, reproduced with permission
10   A private letter, reproduced with permission
11   A private letter, reproduced with permission
12   Fairacres Chronicle
13   First Chapter Charge, 1973
14   A private letter, reproduced with permission
15   Some personal annotations on the Community's Rule, 1989
16   First Chapter Charge, 1973

17 A private letter, reproduced with permission
18 A private letter, reproduced with permission
19 A private letter, reproduced with permission
20 A private letter, reproduced with permission
21 A private letter, reproduced with permission
22 A private letter, reproduced with permission
23 Fairacres Chronicle
24 A private letter, reproduced with permission
25 Fairacres Chronicle
26 A private letter, reproduced with permission
27 A private letter, reproduced with permission
28 A private letter, reproduced with permission
29 A private letter, reproduced with permission
30 A private letter, reproduced with permission
31 A private letter, reproduced with permission

Lightning Source UK Ltd.
Milton Keynes UK
UKOW05n1855290916

284121UK00001B/2/P